OXFORD BOOKWORMS LIBRARY
Classics

The Merchant of Venice

WILLIAM SHAKESPEARE

Stage 5 (1800 ~~headwords~~)

Retold by Clare West
Illustrated by Thomas Girard

Series Editor: Rachel Bladon
Founder Editors: Jennifer Bassett
and Tricia Hedge

OXFORD
UNIVERSITY PRESS

Great Clarendon Street, Oxford, OX2 6DP, United Kingdom

Oxford University Press is a department of the University of Oxford.
It furthers the University's objective of excellence in research, scholarship,
and education by publishing worldwide. Oxford is a registered trade
mark of Oxford University Press in the UK and in certain other countries

This simplified edition © Oxford University Press 2016

The moral rights of the author have been asserted

First published in Oxford Bookworms 2016

10 9 8 7 6 5

No unauthorized photocopying

ISBN: 978 0 19 420971 7   Book
ISBN: 978 0 19 462120 5   Book and audio pack

Printed in China

Word count (main text): 18,470 words

For more information on the Oxford Bookworms Library,
visit www.oup.com/elt/gradedreaders

ACKNOWLEDGEMENTS

To my lovely grandchildren, James and Ava

Illustrations by: *Thomas Girard/Good Illustration.*

The publisher would like to thank the following for their permission to reproduce photographs:
Bridgeman Art Library (Bridge of Sighs, Venice (La Riva degli Schiavoni) c.1740 (oil on canvas),
Canaletto, (Giovanni Antonio Canal) (1697–1768)/Toledo Museum of Art, Ohio, USA/Bridgeman
Images); Corbis (Portrait of William Shakespeare/Antar Dayal/Illustration Works).

Cover: Bridgeman Art Library (The Molo, Venice, Canaletto, (Giovanni Antonio Canal)
(1697–1768)/Private Collection/Photo © Christie's Images/Bridgeman Images).

CONTENTS

PEOPLE IN THIS STORY

In Venice

Antonio a merchant of Venice

Salarino, Solanio, and Gratiano friends of Antonio and
  Bassanio

Bassanio Antonio's friend

Lorenzo a friend of Bassanio and Antonio, in love with
  Jessica

Shylock a rich money-lender

Tubal Shylock's friend

Lancelot Gobbo Shylock's (later Bassanio's) servant

Jessica Shylock's daughter

The Duke of Venice the most important person in Venice

In Belmont

Portia a young lady

Nerissa Portia's maid

The Prince of Morocco } two of Portia's suitors
The Prince of Aragon

Stephano Portia's servant

CHAPTER 1

On the Streets of Venice

My purse, my person, my extremest means,
Lie all unlocked to your occasions.

It was a grey afternoon, and soft rain was falling on the streets and waterways of Venice as three friends made their way slowly towards the Piazza San Marco. The tallest of the three, Antonio, hung his head sadly as they walked, and his two companions watched him with worried expressions on their faces.

'My dear friends,' Antonio said, stopping for a moment to look at both of them, 'I'm very grateful for your concern, I really am. I have no idea why I'm so sad at the moment.'

His friend Salarino put a hand on Antonio's shoulder, and said kindly, 'A merchant's life is full of worry; we all understand that. You have ships out on the oceans, carrying your goods through dangerous waters. It's only natural for your mind to be far away. After all, if your ships went down, all your goods would be lost!'

The other man, Solanio, nodded his head. 'Believe me, Antonio,' he said, 'if so much of *my* wealth was at sea, I'd spend all my time worrying about it. I'd watch the way the wind blows every day, and try to think of safe harbours for my ships in a storm. Any little thing that reminded me of the danger to my ships would make me miserable, I'm sure of it.'

'Exactly!' cried Salarino, eager to add his support. 'If I breathed on my soup to cool it, I'd imagine what harm a strong wind might do at sea. If I saw a stone building, I'd immediately think of the dangerous rocks that might break my ships to pieces. I understand what the problem is, Antonio. You're worried about the goods your ships are carrying.'

'Believe me, no, that's not it,' replied Antonio.

Salarino and Solanio looked at each other in surprise.

'Why, then you're in love!' burst out Solanio, laughing.

'No, Solanio, I'm not in love!' Antonio said with a smile.

Solanio frowned, and paused to think for a moment. 'Not in love?' he said. 'Well then, let's just say the reason you're sad is that you're not happy, and leave it at that!'

'Thank you, my dear friends, for trying to make me feel more cheerful,' replied Antonio.

Just then, they caught sight of three well-dressed gentlemen coming purposefully down the street towards them. 'Look, Antonio,' said Solanio, 'here comes your great friend Bassanio, with Gratiano and Lorenzo.'

For a few moments, all six men stood on the pavement, greeting each other warmly. Then Salarino and Solanio said goodbye and walked away down the street in the light rain. Gratiano and Lorenzo did not stay long either.

'We'll leave you two together,' Lorenzo said to Bassanio and Antonio. 'I know Bassanio wants to talk to you about something, Antonio.'

But as he was turning to walk away, Gratiano said, 'You don't look well, Antonio. You're one of my greatest friends, so I must say this to you. Don't be one of those men who never smile because they want to be seen as wise and deep. It's much better to play the fool and have a face lined from laughter than to let your heart turn cold from sadness—' He stopped speaking suddenly, realizing that Lorenzo had a hand on his arm and was trying to pull him away. 'Ah, I think it's time for us to leave! Well, more of that later, Antonio, when we see you for the party! Goodbye!'

They hurried away down the narrow street. Antonio watched them until they were out of sight, then turned and said to Bassanio with a smile, 'What was that all about?'

'Oh, don't worry about Gratiano!' replied Bassanio lightly. 'You know him. He talks a lot of nonsense. You could spend all day and all night trying to understand what he's talking about and still not make any sense of it! Don't give him another thought.'

The two friends walked on together, and entered the Piazza San Marco. Putting his own worries to one side for a moment, Antonio remembered that Bassanio wanted to talk to him about something. As usual, the square was crowded with people, but they were busy with their own conversations, and Antonio thought it was a good place for a private talk. 'Well then, my friend,' he said, smiling, 'let's talk about *you*. Lorenzo said that there was something you wanted to discuss?'

Bassanio's eyes brightened, and his words came out in a rush. 'Well, I'll have to start at the beginning. Antonio, you know only too well how much money I've spent in recent years – far more than I can afford. How foolish I've been! I can't blame anyone but myself for this. But now my main concern is to pay back everything I've borrowed. I owe the most to you, Antonio, and because we're such good friends, I feel I must explain to you exactly how I hope to get clear of all my debts.'

Antonio stopped walking and turned to look at his friend. 'Go on, my dear Bassanio,' he said encouragingly. 'And if your plan is honourable, as I know you yourself are, then you can be sure I'll help you in every possible way. Just tell me what you need.'

'You can be sure I'll help you in every possible way.'

Bassanio smiled gratefully at Antonio. 'You're very kind, but I must tell you the worst at once. You see, I'm completely unable to repay what I owe you now. And, well…' He hesitated. 'This seems an awful lot to ask, but if you would trust me, and lend me even more, I think I could manage to pay you back, and pay the previous debt, too.'

Antonio put a hand on Bassanio's shoulder, and frowned at him, pretending to be angry. 'But why are you explaining all this to me? You know me well enough to be sure that I'll help you. Just say what you want me to do, and I'll do it!'

Bassanio took a deep breath, and a soft, dreamy expression came into his eyes as he spoke. 'Very well, then. In Belmont, not far from Venice, there's a lady whose name is Portia. She has a large fortune, and she's beautiful, very beautiful. But more importantly, she has every excellent quality known to man. When I met her, she looked at me in a way that gave me hope. But, you see, the whole world has heard of her, and rich and noble men from every country come to ask for her hand in marriage.' He turned to Antonio, and added with feeling, 'If I had the money to compete with them, I feel sure I could win her love!'

Antonio looked at Bassanio thoughtfully for a moment. 'You know that I have spent all my money on goods that are now at sea, so I have nothing to give you at present. But go and see how much you can borrow from one of the money-lenders. Tell them that I sent you – they know that I'll be able to pay them back. I'll go, too, and I'm sure one of us will find someone who can lend us what we need. I'll pay whatever is necessary, so that you can go to Belmont and try your luck with the beautiful Portia.'

Bassanio took Antonio's hand and shook it. 'I can never thank you enough,' he said warmly.

Antonio smiled and waved away his friend's thanks. Then, after saying goodbye to each other, the two men left the crowds in the Piazza San Marco, and set out in different directions through the streets of Venice.

CHAPTER 2

Lady Portia's Suitors

Whiles we shut the gate upon one wooer,
Another knocks at the door.

In a richly furnished room in a large house in Belmont, a lady of great beauty was lying on a seat. 'I tell you, Nerissa,' Lady Portia said with a deep sigh, 'I have to confess, I sometimes feel quite tired of life.'

She was speaking to her pretty maid, who was sitting at her feet. Nerissa was extremely fond of her mistress and understood her feelings very well. But she was a cheerful person herself, with plenty of common sense, and sometimes the lords and ladies she served made her just a little impatient.

'Sweet madam,' she replied as gently as she could, 'you'd certainly be tired of life if you had as much misery as you have good fortune. But I sometimes think people who are too wealthy become as miserable as those who have nothing. So the happiest people must be the ones in the middle, like me – neither rich nor poor.'

Portia smiled at her bright-eyed servant. She always felt better when she talked to Nerissa. 'Sensible thoughts, and well expressed,' she said.

'Well, advice is only any good if it's taken, madam,' said Nerissa.

Privately she was imagining how happy she would be if she had only half of Portia's beauty and wealth. 'I certainly wouldn't ever get tired or depressed!' she thought. 'And if my lady has any sense, she'll realize how lucky she is!'

But Portia had started speaking again. 'Well, it's easy to *know* the right thing to do; it's much harder to actually *do* it. If it was always easy to do the right thing, then the world would be a much better place. Oh, Nerissa!' She put her pale hands to her head, suddenly remembering the reason for her unhappiness.

'What, my lady?' said Nerissa kindly.

'Thinking like this doesn't help me to choose a husband,' she said, adding with a bitter laugh, 'What a word – "choose"! I'm not allowed to choose a man I like, nor refuse one I dislike. The wishes of a living daughter are not as important as the will of a dead father. Don't you think it's hard, Nerissa, that I can neither choose nor refuse a husband?'

Nerissa smiled sympathetically at her mistress. Portia's father had arranged a contest in his will, so that her suitors had to choose from three caskets – gold, silver, and lead – each with a different message on it. Only the suitor who chose the correct casket could marry Portia. 'Your father was a good man, my lady,' Nerissa said, 'and when good men are close to death, they often have good ideas. It's an unusual contest, certainly, but I'm sure the person who chooses correctly will be someone that you can love.'

As she spoke, she was thinking, 'Well, that's what we have to believe. Personally, I know I wouldn't be too pleased if I had to find a husband through a contest like that!' However, she did not give any clue to her thoughts, and simply added, 'But, my lady, how do you feel about any of the lords and princes who have come here so far?'

This question had an excellent effect on Portia, as Nerissa had hoped it would. The lady sat up on her seat and made

herself comfortable, saying quite cheerfully, 'Just run through
their names, dear Nerissa, and I'll tell you.'

'Well, first there's the Prince of Naples,' said Nerissa,
beginning to number Portia's suitors on her fingers.

Her mistress laughed. 'He does nothing but talk of his
horse, and he's very proud of being able to put new shoes on
it himself!'

Nerissa nodded in smiling agreement. 'Then there's the
Count Palatine. How about him?'

'Just run through their names, dear Nerissa, and I'll tell you.'

Portia waved away the mention of his name. 'Oh, he does nothing but frown all the time. Even the most amusing stories and the funniest jokes never make him smile. Just imagine how miserable he'll be when he's old, if he's so cross when he's young! Don't let me marry either of these two men!'

Nerissa took her mistress's hand for a moment, to show her support. 'Well,' she continued, 'what do you think of the French lord, Monsieur Le Bon?'

Portia rolled her eyes upwards to the ceiling. 'He's so worried about trying to be better than everyone else that I have no idea who he actually is! He says he has a better horse than the Prince of Naples, and he frowns more often than the Count Palatine. I've even seen him fight his own shadow! However deeply he loved me, I could never, never love him.'

Nerissa laughed. How right Portia was! But there were still two more names on the list. 'Then what do you say to Falconbridge, the young English lord?'

Portia put her head in her hands. 'You know I can't say anything to him at all, because he doesn't understand me, and I don't understand him! He can't speak Latin, French, or Italian, and I must confess my English is poor. He's the perfect picture of a handsome man, I give you that, but who can make conversation with a picture?'

'How about the Scottish lord, his neighbour?'

'He seems very forgiving. He let the Englishman hit him on the ear, and said only that he would hit him back later. I hope to avoid marrying *him*.'

'You needn't fear, madam,' said Nerissa. Now was the moment to give her mistress some good news. 'All these lords have told me that they're not going to trouble you any more, and are going to return to their countries. They understand the rules of the contest: they know that if they fail, they must swear to leave here at once and never ask another woman to marry them. And they have decided not to take that risk. They all plan to leave, unless your hand in marriage can be won in some other way.'

Portia clapped her hands delightedly, and lay back in her seat, looking calmer. 'I shall only give my hand to the man who wins my father's contest, Nerissa. I'm glad these lords are all so reasonable – because the only thing I love about them is their absence! Let's hope they have safe and pleasant journeys home!'

There was a moment's silence.

'Do you remember, my lady,' Nerissa said hesitantly, 'when your father was alive, a young man from Venice came here? He was a man of learning and a soldier.'

The colour rose in Portia's face. 'Yes, yes,' she replied. 'Now, what was his name... Bassanio, wasn't it?'

Nerissa knew her mistress much too well to believe that she was really unsure of the man's name, but she just smiled and nodded. 'Yes, madam, that was the name. I think that, of all the men I've ever seen, *he* was the one who would most deserve a fine and beautiful lady like you.'

There was a soft expression in Portia's eyes. 'I remember him well,' she confessed. 'And I remember that your good opinion of him is correct.'

A door opened, and a servant entered.

'The five suitors are waiting to say goodbye to you, my lady,' he said. 'And a messenger from the Prince of Morocco says he will be here tonight to enter the contest.'

Portia sighed. 'I wish I could greet the sixth as warmly as I say goodbye to the other five! Come, Nerissa.'

CHAPTER 3

Shylock's Bond

In this there can be no dismay:
My ships come home a month before the day.

One of the wealthiest money-lenders in Venice, Shylock could usually be found on the Rialto, doing business with the merchants. But this afternoon he was walking down a narrow street by the canal with Bassanio. Shylock was a white-haired old man who walked with a stick and kept his head bent low as he talked.

'Three thousand ducats...' he was saying.

'Yes, sir,' said Bassanio, 'for three months.'

'For three months...' repeated Shylock slowly.

'And Antonio will sign a bond, promising to pay the money back to you with interest.'

'Antonio will sign a bond...' Shylock repeated, even more slowly.

Bassanio was becoming impatient. 'What's wrong with the old fool?' he thought. 'Doesn't he understand? Why won't he answer?' But he knew that Shylock was the only man in Venice who could lend him the money he needed for his trip to Belmont. He took a couple of deep breaths, therefore, and then put on an expression of polite enquiry. 'Well, sir, will you agree?' he asked. 'May I know your answer?'

Few things escaped Shylock's notice, and he was immediately aware of the younger man's annoyance. He stopped walking suddenly, so that Bassanio, who had gone on ahead, had to turn back. Shylock smiled secretly to himself.

'Three thousand ducats for three months, and Antonio will sign a bond,' he repeated thoughtfully.

'Yes! What is your answer to that?' Bassanio asked, his voice rising unpleasantly.

Shylock was enjoying himself. His small bright eyes looked up at Bassanio, and he smiled in a friendly way. 'Antonio is a good man,' he said, nodding.

Bassanio's anger was growing inside him. 'What game is this old man playing?' he thought, and he could not stop himself bursting out, 'Have you heard anyone say he isn't?'

Shylock threw up both hands, pretending to be horrified. 'Oh, no, no, no, no! What I meant was that he has enough money to repay this debt. But still...' he waved an ancient finger at Bassanio, 'his goods are in some danger. He has one ship on its way to Tripoli and another to Asia, and I hear now on the Rialto that he has a third going to Mexico, a fourth to England, and business in other parts of the world, too. There are thieves everywhere, on land and at sea, and then there are the dangers of waves, winds, and rocks... However, the man is wealthy enough. Three thousand ducats – hmm... I think I can take his bond.'

Bassanio could not avoid showing his anger. 'I'm sure you can!' he almost spat into Shylock's face.

The old man frowned at this rudeness, and replied, thin-lipped, 'But *I* need to be sure I can, so *I* need to think about it first. May I speak to Antonio?'

'He's on the Rialto,' said Bassanio. 'If you need to speak to him, we can go and find him there.'

The two men turned and walked away down the canal, and soon found Antonio with a group of merchants.

'Let me speak to him first,' Bassanio said to Shylock, and he took his friend Antonio to one side and whispered in his ear for a few moments.

Shylock watched the two men with a long sideways look. 'Antonio!' he thought angrily. 'How I hate that man! He lends his money for nothing, which brings down the interest that I can charge. And then he complains to all the merchants in Venice about me, and tells them that I don't deserve my hard-earned wealth. I can never forgive him for that – and if I ever get the chance, I won't hesitate to destroy him!'

'Shylock!' called Bassanio, breaking into the old man's thoughts. 'Tell us what you think.'

'Antonio! How I hate that man!'

'Young man, I can't put my hand on three thousand ducats at this moment,' said Shylock, with an oily smile. 'But that doesn't matter. I can ask my friend Tubal to provide the cash. How many months was it for again?' He turned politely towards Antonio, saying, 'Good afternoon, Signor Antonio.'

Antonio only nodded his head once, and said coldly, 'Shylock, there is something I must explain. Normally I never lend or borrow money with interest, but this time, just this once, I'm breaking my custom in order to help a friend. Bassanio will need the money for three months.'

'I'd forgotten, ah yes, three months,' said Shylock, smiling innocently. 'Well then, your bond – let me see...' Suddenly he frowned in a puzzled way. 'But wait a minute! I thought you said that you never lend or borrow money with interest?'

Antonio's face was reddening. He knew that the money-lender was deliberately making fun of him. 'I've already explained that to you, Shylock!' he cried angrily. 'Just tell me, can we borrow the money from you or not?'

Shylock's smile returned, but there was no friendliness in it now. 'Signor Antonio,' he said, 'you have said many terrible things about me on the Rialto. You've called me cut-throat, thief, and dog, all because I charge interest on my own money. You have spat on me and kicked me, but now you tell me that you need my help. Well, what shall I say to you? Shall I say, "Noble sir, you spat on me last Wednesday, and for your politeness I'll lend you all the money you like"?'

Antonio stared at him icily. 'I'm likely to call you names again and to spit on you again, too. If you're going to lend this money, don't lend it to me as a friend, but as an enemy. Then, if I break the bond, you can enjoy punishing me.'

Shylock's face brightened and he opened his arms wide.

'Oh, my dear sir, how angry you are! I would like to be friends with you, and forget the hate you've poured on me! I'm ready to lend you the money without taking a penny of interest.'

'That *would* be kind!' said Bassanio, frowning.

'I'll show you how kind I am,' continued Shylock. 'Come with me to a lawyer and sign your bond. And, as a sort of joke, we could say this: if you don't repay me on the day that we agree on, the punishment will be a pound of your flesh, which I can cut off from your body, near your heart. Ha ha!' And the old man laughed so hard that he was almost bent double.

'Fine,' answered Antonio, with a dry smile. 'I'll sign that bond, and tell people that Shylock is kinder than they think.'

'No, Antonio!' cried Bassanio. 'I won't let you sign a bond like this for me! I'd rather not have the money!'

Antonio clapped his friend on the shoulder. 'I won't break the bond, never fear. Within two months I expect my ships to return, bringing me at least nine thousand ducats – that's a whole month before the end of the bond.'

Shylock nodded enthusiastically. 'And anyway, noble Bassanio, if your friend broke the bond, what use would I have for a pound of his flesh? I couldn't sell it, could I? No, believe me, I'm simply making this offer out of kindness.'

'I'll sign the bond, Shylock,' repeated Antonio.

'Then meet me in an hour at the lawyer's,' said Shylock. 'You can go and tell him about this amusing little arrangement of ours! I'll get the ducats, and be with you soon.' He walked off with surprising speed down the street, his stick tapping on the pavement.

'I don't like it, Antonio,' said Bassanio anxiously.

But Antonio put his hand on Bassanio's shoulder. 'Don't worry, Bassanio,' he said. 'There's nothing to be afraid of.'

CHAPTER 4

The Three Caskets

All that glitters is not gold. Often have you heard that told.

It had been raining all afternoon in Belmont, but the skies had now cleared, and the air smelled fresh and cool. Lady Portia was waiting anxiously to welcome another eager suitor to her largest sitting-room, with its shining mirrors, well-chosen furniture, and antique vases full of perfumed flowers. As the double doors from the hall opened, the Prince of Morocco came in, followed by Nerissa. Lady Portia rose at once from her seat in order to greet him.

'My lady,' said the Prince to Portia, 'I have come a long way across the seas, because so many travellers have spoken of your great beauty and your goodness, and I wanted to test the truth of their words for myself. But now that I'm here, I can only say that they painted a poor picture of you. The reality in front of me is far, far lovelier than all the descriptions I've heard.'

Portia looked at him for a moment before answering. Was this the man who would become her husband? She had heard very similar words from all her suitors. 'As you know, fair prince,' she said, giving him her hand with a smile, 'my future is decided by the contest that my father described in his will. But if I had a free choice, I can promise that you would have as good a chance of gaining my love as any of the gentlemen who've come here so far.'

The Prince looked delighted. 'How happy you make me, fair lady!' he said. 'Then let us hope I'll have good fortune when I try my luck in the contest. Perhaps you're aware that I am well-known for my bravery in the field of battle. When in danger, I have no fear. And if I could, I'd fight the strongest enemy or the wildest animal in order to win you, my lady. But, sad to say, in a game of chance the weaker man may win. And so I may lose you to a less deserving man, and then I will... I will die of sadness.'

Portia replied in a voice of warning, 'Remember, you must promise to agree to the rules of the contest. Think carefully before you decide to take your chance.'

The Prince smiled confidently at her. 'I understand and accept the rules,' he replied, nodding. 'I swear to do three things. First, I'll never tell anyone which casket I choose. Next, if I fail, I'll never ask another woman to marry me. Lastly, if I fail, I promise to leave your house at once and never return.'

Portia nodded. 'Every suitor for my hand in marriage has to swear to follow these rules, Prince – you're not alone.'

'Please lead me to the place where the caskets are kept. I am ready now to attempt the contest, which will make me either the happiest or the most miserable of men!'

Portia sighed. 'Come with me, then, Prince,' she said, and led the way through the sitting-room to a small study. At one end of this room, which appeared to have no furniture in it, there was a large curtain of richly-coloured material.

'Nerissa,' said Portia, 'open the curtain.'

Nerissa drew the heavy curtain to one side, and three caskets, placed on three small tables, came into view.

'Now, noble Prince,' said Portia, 'it is time for you to make your choice.'

The Prince paused for a moment. 'My lady Portia,' he said, 'how shall I know if I have chosen the right casket?'

'Now, noble Prince,' said Portia, 'it is time for you to make your choice.'

'One of them contains my picture, Prince,' Portia replied. 'If you choose that one, then I am yours forever.' Her face became pale as she spoke. 'He may think it's an important choice for him,' she was thinking, 'but what about me? My whole life will be in his hands if he chooses the right casket!'

'I can only hope my judgement will be good!' said the Prince, and he stepped forward. 'Let me see... What have we here?' He moved towards the lead casket, and read the message on it aloud:

❖ *'Who chooses me must give and hazard all he has.*

Must give – for what? For lead? Hazard everything for lead? This is a threat. Men who risk everything do it in hope of gaining something precious, not a worthless metal. So I certainly won't give or hazard everything for lead.'

He turned to the silver casket, and bent over it. 'What does the silver casket say?

❖ *Who chooses me shall get as much as he deserves.*

As much as he deserves! I must think about that. How much do I deserve? I do indeed deserve her, because of my noble blood, my wealth, and my good character. But more than these, I deserve her because I love her! What if I looked no further, but chose this one here?'

He hesitated, and looked at the gold casket. 'Let's see what's written on the gold one.

❖ *Who chooses me shall gain what many men desire.*

Why, that's the lady! All the world desires her! Princes come from the four corners of the earth, through deserts and over mountains. Even the wild oceans, with their great waves, winds, and storms, can't stop these men from coming to ask for fair Portia's hand in marriage!'

The Prince was lost in thought, and the small room was very quiet. Nerissa was looking anxiously at her mistress. It was hard to tell what Portia was thinking; her face was perfectly expressionless as she waited.

'Well, well, I must decide,' the Prince said at last. 'One of these three caskets contains her beautiful picture. Is it likely that I will find her inside cheap, dull lead? Surely not! Or is it possible that she's imprisoned in silver, which is ten times less valuable than gold? Oh no! Never could so rich a jewel be buried in anything less than gold! Here inside this casket lies Portia's picture! Give me the key! This is the one I choose!'

Portia took out a small gold key from the pocket of her dress, and handed it to the Prince. 'There, take it, Prince,' she said, 'and if my picture lies within, then I am yours.'

With trembling hands the Prince turned the tiny key in the lock and opened the gold casket. 'Oh no!' he cried in horror, as he looked inside. 'What have we here? The skull of a dead man! And in its empty, lifeless eyes, there's some paper with writing on it! What does it say?'

He took out the paper and read aloud:

❖ *'All that glitters is not gold,*
Often have you heard that told.
Many men their lives have sold
In the search for what I hold.
Wish for gold, and you will die.
A wiser head, a sharper eye,
Would not be reading this reply.
Your journey's over, so goodbye.'

He put his head in his hands. 'I've lost!' he said in a broken voice. 'All my hopes are destroyed!'

After a moment or two, he lifted his head, and looked bravely at Portia. 'My journey is indeed over. Lady Portia, goodbye. My heart is too heavy for me to speak – I shall leave at once.'

He moved slowly towards the door, and departed.

'Well, that's a relief,' said Portia, once the Prince's steps could no longer be heard in the hall. 'Draw the curtain closed, Nerissa. I'm not sure these caskets are going to bring any happiness to anyone, and I'd rather not have to look at them again until it's absolutely necessary.'

Nerissa smiled cheerfully at her mistress. 'Don't worry, my lady,' she said. 'The right suitor will come along soon!'

'I do hope so,' replied Portia.

CHAPTER 5

A Plan of Escape

Farewell, and if my fortune be not crossed,
I have a father, you a daughter, lost.

A mist had come down over Venice, and in the corner of a quiet square near Shylock's house, Gratiano, Salarino, and Lorenzo were standing with their heads close together.

'So, Shylock has lent Bassanio the money he needs, everything is ready for his trip to Belmont – and I am going with him!' Gratiano was saying excitedly.

'You?' said Salarino. 'But you're too wild and loud. Won't you damage Bassanio's chances of winning the contest, and gaining Portia's love?'

'That was exactly what Bassanio said,' Gratiano laughed. 'So I have promised to be the perfect picture of a quiet, polite, serious gentleman.'

Salarino and Lorenzo looked at each other doubtfully.

'But not tonight!' said Gratiano. 'Tonight is Bassanio's masked party, and everyone needs to enjoy themselves. Anyway, Lorenzo,' he said, turning to his friend with a smile, 'didn't I see Shylock's servant Lancelot Gobbo going to your house earlier, with a letter? A letter from Shylock's daughter, the beautiful Jessica, perhaps?'

'You're right,' Lorenzo smiled. 'And I wanted to ask you two for some help. Jessica is so unhappy at her father's house that she can't stay there a minute longer. Everyone in Venice knows how cruel Shylock is to her! He keeps her shut up in that dark house and forbids her to go out. Even his servant Lancelot hates him, and this very afternoon he went to ask Bassanio for a job at his house. He will be Bassanio's servant now.'

'How can we help you, Lorenzo?' asked Salarino.

'Jessica and I love each other,' Lorenzo said. 'We're going to marry and be happy for the rest of our lives. But first I need to get her away from that house.'

'We'll be happy to help you,' said Gratiano.

Lorenzo smiled, and put a hand on each man's shoulder. 'I'm meeting Jessica at her father's house tonight, at supper-time, when it's dark. She's going to disguise herself as a servant boy, and then we can help her to escape.'

'We'll be wearing masks for Bassanio's party, so we'll be in disguise already,' said Gratiano. 'But what about old Shylock himself? We can't rescue the girl from the house if her father's there! And Shylock's so frightened of someone breaking into his house and stealing his money that he hardly ever goes out at night.'

'Ah well, Jessica and I have made a plan,' said Lorenzo excitedly. 'Bassanio is inviting Shylock to the masked party at his house tonight, and we're sure the old man will accept. He's trying to be friends with Bassanio and Antonio, so he really can't refuse.'

'Aha!' said Salarino, laughing. 'Then Shylock's house will be unguarded tonight. The cage will be open, and the bird may fly!'

'It's my dearest wish to set her free,' said Lorenzo softly.

'Then let's meet here in two hours' time, with our masks, and put this plan into action!' said Gratiano heartily.

'My friends, I can never thank you enough for your help!' said Lorenzo.

The three men shook hands, and in a few moments had disappeared into the mist.

⧗

Round the corner, in the dark hall of Shylock's house, Shylock himself was speaking to his young servant, Lancelot Gobbo.

'You're a fool, boy,' the money-lender was saying crossly. 'Going to work for Bassanio, are you? Well, you'll soon see the difference between him and me. *He* won't let you fill your stomach with fine food, as I've done. *He* won't let you sleep all morning, as I've done. *He* won't replace the clothes you've worn and torn.' He turned his head towards the stairs, and called sharply, 'Jessica, come here!'

A door opened and closed above their heads, and Jessica came rapidly downstairs. She was an extremely pretty girl with dark hair.

'Did you call, Father?' she asked obediently. 'What is it?'

'Jessica,' said the old man, 'this foolish boy has decided to serve Bassanio from now on, and he's brought me an invitation to a party at Bassanio's house. I don't know why I've been invited, but Antonio likes to throw his money around, so why not take advantage of him? Here are my keys, Jessica. You'll be responsible for my house and everything in it tonight.' He gave Jessica a number of keys fastened on to a large metal ring, and she put them carefully in her pocket.

'Take good care of the house, my girl,' he said, frowning. 'I have a strong feeling I shouldn't go. Something isn't right. I know, because I dreamed of moneybags last night!'

Lancelot Gobbo had kept silent all this time, but now he was beginning to worry that Shylock might refuse Bassanio's invitation. Knowing how important Shylock's absence from home was, tonight of all nights, he said politely, 'I beg you, sir, do go. My new master expects you to be there. It's going to be a masked party, with singing, and music, and dancing!'

'What?' cried Shylock, horrified. 'Listen to me, Jessica! Lock the door carefully when I've gone, and make sure you stay indoors – and don't look out of the windows at these fools with their masks! Well, I have no wish to go, but I suppose I must. You, boy, go ahead of me and tell Bassanio I'm coming!'

On his way out, Lancelot managed to whisper to Jessica, 'Lorenzo's coming! Look out of the window in two hours' time!'

But Shylock's quick, bright eyes saw what was happening at once. 'What did he say? Tell me, girl, what was it?' he said to his daughter.

'Nothing important, Father,' replied Jessica calmly. 'Just "Goodbye, mistress" – that's all.'

'Well, well, Jessica, as soon as I've gone out, do as I tell you – shut the front door and lock it carefully.'

'Goodbye, Father,' Jessica replied, and she watched him follow Lancelot out into the street. She wondered if it was the last time she would see her father, and was saddened that the thought had no effect on her at all. 'It's so wrong to be ashamed to be my father's child,' she thought. 'But I hate the way he lives. Oh Lorenzo, if you keep your promises, I shall soon be free – and your loving wife.'

She breathed a sigh of relief as she closed the heavy front door, and hurried upstairs. There was plenty for her to do.

'First, my disguise!' she told herself. She unlocked a cupboard in her bedroom, where she had hidden the servant clothes that Lancelot had brought for her the day before. She put the clothes on and looked at herself in a mirror. 'I make a very good servant boy!' she thought, smiling at her reflection.

Then she packed some of her dresses in a box, with several pairs of shoes, her hairbrushes, her perfume, and two of her favourite books.

There was one last thing she had been thinking about doing. But now that the moment had come, she was not sure whether to or not. She walked slowly out of her bedroom and went downstairs to her father's private office. Using one of the keys on the ring he had given her, she unlocked the door and went in. Another key opened the cupboard under his desk; she knew this was where he kept the jewellery that her mother had worn when she was alive.

She took out the jewellery and looked at it – a pretty silver ring, a heavy gold necklace and matching bracelet, and two large, uncut diamonds. 'I'm sure I can take them,' she told herself. 'After all, he always said that he would give them to me on my wedding day, if I married someone that he'd chosen. So in a way they belong to me.'

Then she saw two heavy bags of coins in the same cupboard, and after hesitating a moment, she took them as well. She wrapped the jewels carefully and, returning to her bedroom, added them to the box, which she closed and locked. Now all she had to do was wait.

It seemed a long time before she heard footsteps below her window, and a man's voice calling softly to her.

'Lorenzo!' she cried, as she rushed to open the window and put her head out. In the street she could see two dark figures holding torches, and Lorenzo's smiling face looking up at her.

'Jessica!' he whispered, as loudly as he dared. 'Are you ready?'

'I am,' she replied, adding with a nervous laugh, 'I'm glad it's dark and you can't see me in these clothes!' She threw the two bags of ducats out of the window.

Jessica threw the two bags of ducats out of the window.

Lorenzo passed them to the dark figures and then called, 'Come down and open the door, Jessica, as fast as you can. There's no time to lose. We have a boat waiting for us at the harbour – you and I are going straight there. You'll pretend to be my servant, carrying a torch. Gratiano and Salarino will go to the party at Bassanio's house.'

In a few minutes, he could hear footsteps. The front door opened, and Jessica stood there with her box. She ran into his arms.

'I'm giving up everything for you, Lorenzo!' she sobbed tearfully. 'Will you always love me and take care of me?'

'My dearest one,' he replied, 'how could I do anything else? You're wise and beautiful and true, and I'll love you till my dying day. But what's in these bags, and in this box?'

'My father's ducats, and my mother's jewels,' said Jessica, smiling through her tears. 'I think I deserve them after all his cruelty to me. We can consider them his wedding gift to us!'

With Salarino and Gratiano's help, the young couple hurried off together into the darkness. Lorenzo's two friends were shaking hands, congratulating each other on a job well done, when they heard a voice behind them.

'Gratiano! Where are you?'

'Signor Antonio!' said Gratiano, recognizing the merchant's voice.

'Ah, there you are!' cried Antonio. 'I've been looking everywhere for you. The party at Bassanio's is cancelled – the wind has changed direction and is perfect for sailing. Come to the harbour as fast as you can. You and Bassanio will be leaving for Belmont tonight!'

CHAPTER 6

At the Harbour

⌛

Justice! The law! My ducats, and my daughter!

It was now midnight in Venice, and the mist had lifted. Although most of the city's people were in their beds, the harbour was surprisingly busy. A large sailing ship was being prepared for departure, and Bassanio and Gratiano were waiting to board it.

Antonio came to join them. 'It's time for you to leave, my friends,' he said. 'Look, the ship's captain is signalling that he wants to set sail at once.'

'Good luck with the beautiful Lady Portia!' Salarino said, shaking hands first with Bassanio, and then with Gratiano. 'We hope to see you back here soon, Bassanio, with a smile on your face, and a wedding to arrange! Don't forget to invite us!'

'Thank you, my friends,' replied Bassanio. He turned to Antonio. 'I'll be back very soon, with the money to repay you,' he said.

'Don't hurry back for me,' Antonio replied, shaking his head. '*Love* is what you should be thinking of, not Shylock's bond – enjoy yourself, and stay as long as you need to.'

There was a tear in his eye as he took Bassanio's hand and shook it warmly. The two men stood together in silence for a moment. Then Bassanio boarded the ship with his new servant Lancelot Gobbo, followed by Gratiano. The captain gave orders to his men, and the ship sailed slowly away.

Suddenly, shouting was heard. Antonio and Salarino looked

at each other in surprise as Shylock appeared round the corner, running as fast as he could, his white hair blowing wildly in the wind and his lined face red with anger.

'Stop them!' screamed Shylock. 'My ducats! My daughter! She's run away with a young man and stolen my ducats! Not one bag, but two bags – two bags, I tell you! And jewels – two huge stones, two rich and precious stones! Find the girl! She has the stones on her, and the ducats!'

At that moment, a group of the Duke of Venice's soldiers marched into the harbour, followed by the Duke himself.

'Calm down, Shylock,' said the Duke. 'You have woken me to bring me here in search of your daughter, but I see no sign of her. There is a sailing ship in the distance – can anyone tell me who is on that ship?'

'My daughter! My daughter!' shouted Shylock, waving his arms in the air. 'Stop the ship and bring her back!'

Antonio stepped forward and spoke to the Duke. 'Sir, my dear friend Bassanio is on that ship. He's travelling to Belmont, on personal business. I've just said goodbye to him, so I know exactly who's with him. I swear to you that this man's daughter was not on that ship.'

'Thank you, Antonio,' replied the Duke. 'You're one of our most honourable merchants, and therefore I am happy to accept your word. Can you tell me, then, where Shylock's daughter is now?'

'Well, sir,' said Antonio, 'I understand that she left the harbour in a boat with a young man called Lorenzo, about two hours ago.'

'Too late!' cried Shylock. 'We've arrived too late!'

'And early tomorrow morning they'll be married, sir,' Antonio went on.

'Ah!' screamed Shylock, falling to the ground. 'A knife in my heart! No daughter, no stones, no ducats! Justice! I demand justice!'

'I don't think anyone is to blame here,' said the Duke, 'except you, Shylock. Everyone knew how unkind you were to your daughter.' He turned to his soldiers. 'Carry this man back to his house. Be gentle with him; he's had a bad shock.'

The men did as they were told, and Shylock's cries slowly became more and more distant, until the harbour was peaceful once more.

'Justice! I demand justice!'

CHAPTER 7

The Prince of Aragon

҈

With one fool's head I came to woo,
But I go away with two.

'Well, Nerissa, I have yet another suitor eager to attempt the contest.' Portia sighed as she spoke. The windows in her sitting-room were open, letting in the warm spring air from the garden in Belmont.

'Is it the Prince of Aragon, madam?' asked Nerissa.

'Yes, that's right. He's of noble blood, of course, but I know nothing else about him. If he makes a clever choice, I'll have to marry him – and I will only find out what he's really like then. Oh, here he comes, Nerissa.'

The Prince entered the sitting-room.

'You are welcome, noble Prince,' Portia said. 'The caskets are in my study. If you choose the one which contains my picture, then I will marry you at once. But if you fail, you must leave here immediately, and never marry another woman. Those are the rules of my father's contest.'

'I understand, my lady,' the Prince replied, smiling. 'I must now hope for great fortune as I make my choice!'

He followed Portia and Nerissa to the small study, where the heavy curtain had been pulled back, and the three caskets could be seen. He walked slowly up to them.

'I see that the caskets are made of gold, of silver, and of lead,' he said. 'What does the lead casket say?

❧ *Who chooses me must give and hazard all he has.*

I don't want to give or risk everything, just for a casket made of lead! What about the golden casket? Let me see.

❖ *Who chooses me shall gain what many men desire.*

Ha! What many men desire! That "many" might mean most people, who are foolishly deceived by appearances – they don't understand that what's *inside* is more important. I refuse to choose what many men desire – I won't just follow the crowd blindly. So, then, to the silver casket!

❖ *Who chooses me shall get as much as he deserves.*

And well said, too! Only those who are really deserving should reach the highest positions in our society. So much influence can be bought by bribery these days, but that's quite wrong – every honour should be truly deserved.'

He thought to himself for a moment, then smiled confidently at Portia. 'I'm sure I do deserve the best. Lady Portia, give me a key for this silver casket, and I will unlock my fortune.'

Without speaking, Portia took a tiny silver key from her pocket, and handed it to the Prince. He opened the casket, but as he looked inside, his confident smile disappeared. There was an uneasy silence in the small room.

At last, the Prince spoke. He was shaking with anger.

'What's this? The picture of a fool, a madman! This fool's head is nothing like yours, my beautiful lady! This is not what I had dreamed of! Do I deserve no more than a fool's head? Is that my prize? Do I deserve nothing better than that?'

'Prince,' replied Portia calmly, 'don't try to judge whether your failure is just or not.'

Frowning, the Prince turned back to the casket. 'What does it say?'

He read the words on the back of the picture aloud:

❖ *'Welcome to the silver chest!*
Lords have come from east and west,
Their bravery and their skill to test.
There are fools alive, you know,
With silver coat – it's just for show.
You will not take a wife today,
This fool's head is here to stay.
So goodbye; no more to say.'

The Prince's face was pale as he looked up. 'If I stay here any longer, I'll appear an even greater fool. My own foolish head brought me here as a suitor for you, Lady Portia, but now I go away with two fool's heads! Sweet lady, goodbye!'

And with that, the Prince walked rapidly out of the study.

'Draw the curtain, Nerissa,' said Portia, with a sigh of relief. 'How hard these suitors try to win the contest! And how lucky for me that they always make the wrong choice!'

'What will be, will be, madam,' answered Nerissa. She had been looking out of the window, and turned towards her mistress with a wide smile. 'And in fact, madam, I see that someone has arrived at your gate. The young gentleman from Venice who we mentioned the other day, with his servant and a friend of his. He's such a handsome young man! I wonder why he's come?'

Portia's eyes brightened, and she hurried quickly to the window and looked out. Then, when she felt Nerissa's eyes on her, she turned away. 'You make me think he must be some relation of yours, Nerissa, since you talk so highly of him,' she said. 'Well, go and bring him to me.'

Portia returned to her sitting-room to receive Bassanio. On the way, she checked her appearance in a mirror. Suddenly, she felt light-hearted and carefree. 'Perhaps there's a chance of happiness for me after all!' she thought to herself.

CHAPTER 8

Revenge

If you poison us, do we not die?
And if you wrong us, shall we not revenge?

Far from Belmont, bad news had reached the Rialto in Venice, and it was this that Salarino and Solanio were discussing as they walked beside the Grand Canal one afternoon.

'People say that one of Antonio's ships has gone down off the coast of England,' Salarino was telling his friend.

'If that's true, it would mean a serious loss for Antonio,' said Solanio, looking worried. 'That ship of his was full of valuable goods.'

'Well, if he *has* lost one ship, let's just hope the others make it home safely,' said Salarino.

Shylock had turned into the street that Salarino and Solanio were walking along, and the two friends looked at each other as he came towards them.

'I haven't seen him since Lorenzo and Jessica ran away,' said Solanio.

'No,' said Salarino, laughing. 'Not since he ran through the streets crying about the money and jewels Jessica had taken from him. Now all the boys in Venice follow him through the city, throwing stones and shouting, "His jewels, his daughter, and his ducats!" '

Shylock had nearly reached them by now, so they stopped laughing and turned towards him politely.

'Good morning, Shylock!' said Solanio. 'What news is

there from the merchants? Tell us, have you heard anything of Antonio?'

The moment Shylock heard the name Antonio, he threw his hands up in the air. 'It was a mistake to lend *him* money! Antonio, who once lent his money so freely, who was always so pleased with himself, has now fallen into debt! Well, he needs to remember that we have a bond.'

'What do you mean, Shylock?' said Salarino. 'I heard that the punishment in the bond if Antonio can't repay you is a pound of his flesh. What's *that* good for?'

Shylock gave an evil laugh. 'To feed fish with! And to feed my revenge! He has made me lose money, he has laughed at both my losses and my gains, he has turned my friends against me and made my enemies hate me more. I have feelings, just like you. If you hurt me, I will bleed. If you poison me, I will die. And if you wrong me, I will take my revenge!'

Salarino and Solanio were too shocked to reply, and they were staring open-mouthed at Shylock when a servant came running up to them with a message. 'Gentlemen,' he said breathlessly, 'my master Antonio is at his house and would like to see you both there.'

'We'll come at once,' replied Salarino.

Without a word to Shylock, the two gentlemen hurried off down the street behind Antonio's servant. As soon as they had disappeared, a small bald-headed man, who had been waiting out of sight nearby, walked quickly up to greet Shylock.

'Ah, Tubal!' said Shylock. 'You're back from Genoa! Have you found my daughter?'

'I met several people who had seen her, but sadly, no, I haven't found her,' the small man replied.

Shylock held his head in his hands and sobbed. 'What pain!

What suffering! One of those diamonds cost me two thousand ducats in Frankfurt. Two thousand ducats in one stone, Tubal, and other precious, precious jewels! I wish my daughter was dead at my feet, and the jewels in her ear! I wish she was laid in her burial clothes, and the ducats laid beside her! I daren't think how much I'm spending on the search – it's one loss on top of another! And still no result, no revenge! The only person suffering here is *me* – all the misfortune falls on *my* shoulders!'

'But you're wrong there, Shylock,' Tubal said quietly. 'Other men have bad luck, too. Antonio, as I heard in Genoa—'

'What?' sobbed Shylock, raising his head and letting the tears dry on his lined face. 'Bad luck? Tell me more, Tubal!'

'Well, one of Antonio's ships has sunk, coming from Tripoli.'

Shylock said nothing for a moment, but a smile moved slowly across his lips. 'Then he has lost even more than I thought and I *shall* have my revenge,' he said quietly. 'Is it true? Are you sure?'

Tubal nodded. 'Some merchants who I met swore to me that Antonio is a ruined man.'

'I'm very glad of it!' cried Shylock, raising his head and smiling unpleasantly. 'I'll make his life a misery. I'm very glad of it!'

Tubal cleared his throat. 'But the same merchants also told me that in one night your daughter spent eighty ducats in Genoa.'

Shylock's smile disappeared and he put his head in his hands again. 'That's like a knife in my heart, Tubal!' he cried. 'Eighty ducats in one night, eighty ducats! I'll never see my gold again!'

'One of them showed me a ring that he bought from your daughter. And what did he give her for it? A monkey!'

'Evil girl! Tubal, that was my dear wife's ring. She gave it to me before we were married! I would not have sold it for five thousand monkeys!'

'But Antonio is certainly ruined,' Tubal said encouragingly.

Shylock's face cleared for a moment. 'That's true; that's very true,' he said, rubbing his hands together. 'Well, Tubal, go and find one of the Duke's officers. Tell him I'll need him when the date of the repayment comes. By then we'll know for sure how many losses Antonio has suffered.'

'What will you do if he breaks his bond?' enquired Tubal.

'I'll tell you what I'll do!' Shylock nodded several times to show his determination. 'I shall have my pound of flesh if he breaks his bond! What do you think of that, eh, Tubal?'

'Business would certainly be easier for you here in Venice without Antonio,' Tubal said.

'Of course you agree with me, my friend! I'll claim justice from the Duke. Well, go, good Tubal, and come to see me later at my house if you have anything more to report to me.'

The little bald-headed man walked with short steps towards the Duke's palace, while Shylock stayed for a moment on the Rialto Bridge. Some small boys began to gather nearby, picking up stones, but the money-lender was so deep in his thoughts that he did not even notice them.

CHAPTER 9

Bassanio's Choice

☙

Let me choose:
For as I am, I live upon the rack.

Bassanio had been in Belmont for some time now, and every day, as he and Portia walked, talked, and laughed together, their feelings drew them closer to each other. But there were two other people in the house who were also thinking of love.

'If my lady had a free choice, I know who she'd choose to marry!' Nerissa said to Gratiano one day, as they watched Bassanio and Portia from a distance.

'Well, *I* have a free choice, and I know who *I'd* choose!' replied Gratiano.

'You've spoken to me of this before. What do you mean by it?' said Nerissa.

'You know very well what I mean,' answered Gratiano. 'Ever since I arrived here with Bassanio, I've only had eyes for you. There's no lovelier girl in the whole of Italy, and no one with such intelligence and common sense as you. I love you from the bottom of my heart, and I swear I always will!'

'A girl has to be careful who she trusts,' Nerissa replied. 'How do I know I can believe you?'

Gratiano went down on one knee and looked up at her. 'Marry me, my sweet Nerissa, and you'll see! I promise I'll love you until my dying day!'

Nerissa considered for a moment. 'I *may* accept you, sir,' she said, smiling down at the young man. He jumped delightedly to his feet and was about to take her in his arms, but she put out a hand to stop him. 'As I was saying,' she continued, 'I *may* accept you. It all depends on my mistress.'

'Ah yes!' cried Gratiano, with sudden understanding. 'You mean, if my friend Bassanio wins the contest…'

'Exactly! If he marries my lady, then I'll be free to get married myself.'

'And you might choose me as your husband?'

Nerissa's face was pink and she was hiding a smile. 'I think I might,' she whispered.

'Say you will! Say yes!'

'Oh, you give a girl no peace! All right then, yes!'

And the happy couple walked away into the garden, arm in arm, discussing their future together.

At last, Bassanio decided that the contest could not be put off any longer, and one day he asked Portia, Gratiano, and Nerissa to meet him in Portia's sitting-room.

Sunshine poured in through the long windows and turned Portia's hair to gold. Bassanio took her hand and said quietly, 'My lady, the time has come for me to make my choice.'

Portia held his hand tightly in both of hers. There was deep anxiety in her voice as she replied, 'My dear Bassanio, please wait a little before you attempt the contest. If you make the wrong choice, you'll have to leave, and something tells me that I really don't want to lose you. I know a woman shouldn't make her feelings quite so clear, but please, stay another month or two before you try to choose the right casket. Perhaps I could teach you how to make the right choice!' She paused for a moment, frowning. 'But no, I have sworn not to do that. And so you might get it wrong. Then if you do, you'll make me wish I'd broken my promise. Oh, how difficult it all is!'

Still holding his hand in hers, she took a step forward and looked up into his face. 'I must tell you – I can't stop myself – I am all yours, whatever fortune may decide!' She let his hand go and turned away with a sigh. 'I'm talking too much, I know, but I'm doing it to put off the awful moment when you attempt the contest!'

'Let me make my choice, sweet Portia!' Bassanio begged desperately. 'I can't wait any longer! It's so painful not knowing whether you'll be mine, or whether some other man will win you! I'm too afraid to enjoy my love for you, in case I lose the contest and we're separated for ever. So lead me to the caskets and let us both hope for success!'

Portia hesitated for a moment and then took a deep breath. 'Well, I suppose the time has come,' she said. 'Follow me, then!' She led the way through the room to the small study, where the heavy curtain was already drawn back.

'Here are the caskets, Bassanio,' Portia said. 'My picture is locked inside one of them, and if you really love me, you will find it. Gratiano, Nerissa, we'll wait and watch. Let's have some music playing while Bassanio chooses. Nerissa, bring in the musicians, will you? They're waiting in the hall. If Bassanio fails to choose correctly, there will be dying notes of music as our hopes are destroyed and our hearts break. But if he wins the contest, the music will give a suitable welcome for a husband to his wedding!'

Nerissa left the room and returned in a few minutes, bringing in a group of musicians.

'Now, Bassanio,' said Portia, 'think carefully and make your choice. For me, it's much, much harder – I have to watch and wait while you fight the battle for me!'

Nerissa moved silently nearer to Portia, and held her mistress's trembling hand. Bassanio walked up to the caskets, but he was looking at the musicians, especially the singer, who stepped forward confidently and sang:

'Tell me, where is Fancy bred,
In the heart, or in the head?
How is it made, how is it fed?
It is created in the eyes,
With looks and stares, and Fancy dies
Where it was born, and there it lies.
I am here these words to tell;
Be sure you note my message well.'

When the song was over, there was silence for a moment. Portia's eyes were fixed on Bassanio's face.

He was considering. 'Hmm...' he said, partly to himself and partly to the others. 'The song is interesting. "Fancy" – that false, shallow feeling when a man's eyes follow a pretty girl down the street, or a woman watches a handsome young man from her window. Fancy is nothing like the deep love I feel for Lady Portia. I think the song must be giving me a warning – don't be deceived by appearances, that's what it's telling me. I'll remember that when I make my choice. It's very true – how often the world is deceived by outward show! How many criminals have hidden the evil things they have done, using fine words to argue their innocence? How many soldiers talk proudly of their brave adventures, in order to cover up their weakness?'

'I think the song must be giving me a warning.'

Portia and her maid looked at each other. Something passed between them – a half-smile, a small nod – and then they turned to look at Bassanio again. Gratiano noticed this wordless communication between the two women, and although he did not understand it, he took it as a hopeful sign. Bassanio himself was concentrating too hard on his thoughts to be aware of what was going on in the room.

'And then there's beauty!' he continued. 'Many women buy false hair to make themselves look beautiful. But that lovely golden hair, blowing lightly in the wind, has often been taken from the head of one who has died, whose body now lies in a grave. Things which appear pretty at first sight may not be what they seem.'

He turned to the three caskets and examined them, reading the message on each one carefully.

'Well, bright and shiny gold, I don't think I will choose you. Nor you, pale silver, which common coins are made of. Now what do I remember of the song – how did it start? *Where is Fancy bred? In the head? How is it fed?* Bred, head, fed... lead. I wonder if that's a clue...'

He paused for a moment, then put his hand on the lead casket.

'Yes, I'll choose you, plain lead, because you promise nothing. You have a plainness which moves me more than these grander metals. Let's hope my choice will bring happiness!'

Portia turned to Nerissa with tears in her eyes and a hand on her heart. 'Perhaps this sudden happiness will be too much for me,' she whispered to her maid. 'Love is so strong – it makes all other feelings disappear! Here is the lead key – give it to him.'

CHAPTER 10

News from Venice

Here is a letter, lady,
The paper as the body of my friend,
And every word in it a gaping wound.

Bassanio took the small key from Nerissa and opened the lead casket. 'What do I find here?' he cried. 'A picture of fair Portia! How beautifully the artist has painted her eyes, her lips, her hair! I cannot speak highly enough of it, but it is only a shadow of the real, living Portia. No painter could ever truly show her loveliness. And here's some paper, which tells me my fortune.'

He paused for a moment, looking at Portia, and then read aloud:

✤ *'You did not choose by looks alone,*
But followed what you've always known.
Since this fortune comes to you,
There is no more you have to do.
Take sweet Portia as your wife,
And happiness is yours for life.'

Bassanio lifted his eyes from the piece of paper and looked straight at Portia. 'Fair lady, I stand here before you, still doubting whether I can really have gained this great prize. And I will not believe that what I have read is true until *you* say that it is.'

Portia looked lovingly at him through her tears. 'You see me, Lord Bassanio, as I am: a simple, inexperienced girl, but one who is young enough and clever enough to learn. I give myself to you, and everything I own is now yours. I have been the lady of this house, mistress of my servants, and queen over myself, but now this house, these servants, and this same self are yours!' She pulled a heavy gold ring off one of her fingers, and held it out to him. 'I give them to you with this ring. Take it and keep it safe, because if you lose it or give it away, it will mean the end of your love for me.'

Bassanio was extremely moved. He took the ring and put it immediately on the fourth finger of his left hand. 'Madam,' he said, 'I don't know what to say. I only know what I *feel*, in my blood and my bones. Your words have filled me with happiness. And I can promise you that this ring will not leave my finger until I am dead.'

Nerissa stepped eagerly forward. 'Now it's time for us to congratulate you with all our hearts! This is just what we've been hoping and wishing for!'

Gratiano came forward too, and shook Bassanio warmly by the hand. 'My dear Bassanio and my gentle lady, I wish you all the happiness that you could possibly desire,' he said, adding with a smile, 'and when you arrange your wedding, I beg you to let me be married at the same ceremony.'

Bassanio clapped his hands in pleasure, laughing. 'Of course, Gratiano, if you can find a wife.'

'Thank you, but you have already found one for me,' said Gratiano. 'You had eyes only for Lady Portia, and my eyes were caught by her maid, Nerissa. You fell in love, and I fell in love, too. And like you, I have lost no time. I have made endless promises of love to Nerissa, and at last she agreed that I could gain her love if you gained her mistress.'

Portia turned to her maid in great surprise. 'Is this true, Nerissa?' she asked.

Smiling shyly, Nerissa replied, 'It is, madam, as long as you're in agreement.'

'And are you serious about this, Gratiano? Do you intend to marry Nerissa?' asked Bassanio.

'I certainly do,' replied Gratiano.

Bassanio looked at Portia, then clapped Gratiano delightedly on the back. 'Well, it would be an honour for Lady Portia and me if you would be married with us,' he said, smiling.

Suddenly voices were heard in the hall. The door opened, and a servant showed Lorenzo, Jessica, and Salarino into the study.

'My dear friends!' cried Bassanio. 'What a wonderful surprise! Welcome to Belmont!' Turning to Portia, he said, 'These are two friends of mine from Venice, Lorenzo and Salarino, and this is Lorenzo's young wife Jessica.'

'As friends of yours,' said Portia, smiling, 'they're very welcome.'

But as they greeted the visitors, they both noticed a darkness in their faces.

'Thank you, my lady,' replied Lorenzo, 'but I fear you may not be so happy, Bassanio, when you hear the reason for our visit. Jessica and I weren't planning to disturb you here, but by chance we met Salarino, who was on his way here from Venice with an important letter for you. You must read it at once. It's from Antonio.'

'Ah, good Antonio!' cried Gratiano. 'What a fine man he is! I know he'll be glad to hear our good news.'

'I think he'd be glad to have a little good news himself,' said Salarino, looking serious. He stepped forward and handed the letter to Bassanio, who opened it at once. As he read and re-read it, his face turned white.

'See how pale he is!' Portia whispered to Nerissa. 'Has some dear friend of his died? What else could it be?' She said aloud, 'Bassanio, tell me the worst. I want to share the troubles this letter brings you.'

Bassanio's face was full of pain as he looked at her. 'Sweet Portia, these are some of the most terrible words that have ever been written. My lady, when I first spoke to you of love, I explained that I had no wealth, that I was a gentleman, nothing more. Perhaps I claimed too much. I should have told you that I had less than nothing, because in fact I'm deep in debt, to my dearest, closest friend, who borrowed money from his bitterest enemy to help me. And now this letter tells me that my friend is in terrible danger. But, Salarino, is it true? Have *all* his ships sunk?'

'Not a single ship has arrived home safely,' replied Salarino, 'so Antonio doesn't have enough money to repay the bond. But Shylock would now refuse to take the money anyway. I've never known a man so determined to destroy someone. He has told the Duke again and again that by the laws of our city, he must have justice. Twenty of the leading merchants, and the Duke himself, have all begged Shylock to reconsider, but he demands for Antonio the punishment that was written into his bond!'

'My father has always hated Antonio,' said Jessica. 'And I know he will make things very difficult for him.'

'How much does your friend Antonio owe this money-lender?' Portia asked Bassanio.

'Three thousand ducats – that's what he borrowed for me.'

'Is that all?' Portia's face lit up, and she gently took Bassanio's arm. 'Pay him six thousand, and destroy the bond! Double six thousand, and then three times that figure, before such a dear friend shall lose a hair through your fault. First, we'll get married, and then you'll go to Venice, with gold to pay this miserable debt twenty times over. Nerissa and I will wait for your return. Come, my love, this is your wedding day! Give your friends a proper welcome, and try to be cheerful.'

But looking at Bassanio's face, Portia could see at once that there was no hope of cheer in his heart. 'Let me hear your friend's letter,' she said softly, taking his hand.

Bassanio smiled sadly at her as he started reading:

> '*My friend Bassanio, my ships have all sunk, and I was not able to repay Shylock in time. And since, in paying the bond, it is impossible for me to live, all debts are cleared between you and me. I ask only that I might be able to see you at my death. But please decide this for yourself. Come only if your feelings for me as a friend persuade you to – and not because of this letter.*'

Portia was crying as he finished reading. 'Oh, my love, now I understand why you are so miserable! Please, get through all your business here and go at once!'

Bassanio looked at her. 'Since you are happy for me to go away, my sweet, I will hurry to Antonio as soon as we have been married. But be in no doubt, I shall not sleep until I am back at your side.'

CHAPTER 11

Portia's Plan

I never did repent for doing good,
Nor shall not now.

That same evening, there was a double wedding in Belmont – a simple ceremony, in which Portia was married to Bassanio, and Nerissa to Gratiano. Early next morning, the two women waved a fond goodbye to their new husbands, who sailed away from Belmont harbour towards Venice.

Lorenzo, Jessica, and Salarino had spent the night at Portia's house as her guests, and as Portia and Nerissa returned from the harbour, Lorenzo and his wife came out into the garden to greet them.

'Madam,' said Lorenzo, 'it's extremely noble and generous of you to provide so much help for your husband's dear friend Antonio. If you only knew what an honourable gentleman Antonio is, and how much he loves your husband, you would be pleased that you have shown such kindness.'

'Thank you, Lorenzo,' replied Portia with a smile, 'I'm always glad to help people. Friends often have similar qualities of character, so I expect that this Antonio must be very like my husband. I'm happy, therefore, to rescue a reflection of my husband from such evil cruelty!'

She paused, then said in a more businesslike manner, 'Lorenzo, Jessica, I've decided I want to be somewhere quiet while Bassanio is away. So Nerissa and I are going to stay in a small place not far from here, until our husbands return. We

That same evening, there was a double wedding in Belmont.

will leave at once. Therefore, I'd like to ask you to look after my house. Please don't refuse – I wouldn't ask unless it was really necessary. Will you take my keys?'

This came as a great surprise to Lorenzo and Jessica, but they took the heavy keys from her, and Lorenzo said politely, 'Madam, with all our hearts, we shall follow your orders. Don't worry, your house will be quite safe in our care.'

'Good,' said Portia. 'That's organized, then. My servants already know my intention, and they will serve you and Jessica. Goodbye, until we meet again!'

'My lady, I wish you a pleasant time away,' added Jessica, and then she and Lorenzo went back into the house.

Nerissa was puzzled, but she knew Portia well enough to understand that her mistress had a plan, although she still had no idea what it might involve.

Portia called her servant Stephano, who soon appeared. 'What can I do for you, my lady?' he enquired.

'Stephano,' replied Portia, 'you have always been honest and true, so I am trusting you to help me now.' She pulled out a piece of paper from the pocket of her dress. 'Here, take this letter and travel at once to the home of my cousin, Doctor Bellario, in Padua. Take whatever notes and clothes he may give you, and bring them with all possible speed to the harbour for the public ferry to Venice. I'll be waiting for you there.'

'I shall go as fast as I can,' said Stephano, and he put the letter carefully in the inside pocket of his coat, and walked quickly back towards the house.

Portia took Nerissa's hand with a playful smile. 'Come, Nerissa,' she said, 'we have work to do. We'll see our husbands in a very short time, but they won't recognize us!'

'Why not, madam?'

'We're going to put on men's clothes, and change ourselves into handsome young men! I tell you, I'm going to make a great man: I'll walk with big strong steps, and tell stories of fights with knives, and of ladies in love with me! Come with me. I'll explain it all to you when we're in my coach, which is waiting for us at the garden gate. We must hurry, because we have to travel a long way today!'

Soon Jessica, who was standing at the sitting-room window, saw Portia's coach and horses drive rapidly away. In a few minutes Lorenzo entered the room.

'Good evening, my lady!' he said with a smile. 'Would you care to give your orders to the servants for my dinner, my lady? Or perhaps you'd wish *me* to do it, my lady?'

'No, no, do let me!' replied Jessica with a laugh. 'But honestly, Lorenzo, what a beautiful house!'

'Very true, my sweet – just right for a fine lady like yourself. But tell me, Jessica, what's your opinion of Bassanio's wife?'

'Oh, I like her so much! How lucky that she and Bassanio have found each other! No other woman alive could possibly match her beauty, her intelligence, and her manners!'

Lorenzo smiled at her enthusiastic words. 'Oh, I love you so much! How lucky that you and I have found each other! You see, your husband is just as perfect as Bassanio's perfect wife! Come, say you agree with me.'

'I'll tell you my opinion later,' replied Jessica with a laugh. 'Now it's time to give orders to the servants for dinner, I seem to remember!'

CHAPTER 12

Antonio on Trial

🛡

The quality of mercy is not strained:
It droppeth as the gentle rain...
Upon the place beneath.

On the morning of Antonio's trial, a large crowd was gathered in the Piazza San Marco, outside the Duke's palace.

In the courtroom inside, Bassanio and Gratiano were waiting for the trial to begin. Two court officials brought Antonio into the room, and as he walked to his seat, Bassanio could see that his face was pale, and his head bent low.

Bassanio was deeply saddened by his friend's appearance. He waved at Antonio, who lifted his head a little and gave a weak smile. Then the Duke entered.

'All rise! All rise for the Duke!' said the chief court official loudly, and everyone stood up. The Duke took his seat in the judge's chair on a raised platform, from where he had a view of the whole courtroom.

'Sit down, sit down,' the Duke said. 'Let's get started. Is the merchant Antonio here?'

'I am here,' Antonio said quietly.

The Duke smiled kindly at him. 'I'm sorry about this, Antonio. You have come up against a cold-hearted man – an inhuman creature, incapable of pity.'

Antonio looked up at the Duke. 'I've heard how hard you've tried to persuade Shylock to cancel our bond, and I'm very grateful. But since he's so determined, and there is nothing more that the law can do to help me, I am resigned to my punishment.'

The Duke nodded, and gave orders for Shylock to be brought before him. The old man walked quickly in and stood in front of the Duke. There was an evil smile on his lined face.

'Shylock,' began the Duke, 'everybody thinks, and so do I, that at the last moment you'll show mercy, instead of cruelty. We believe that you'll not only cancel the punishment, which is to take a pound of this poor merchant's flesh, but also set him free from some of his debt to you. He's had so many losses in the last few months. We all expect you to be generous, Shylock.'

Shylock's evil smile grew wider as he lifted his head to reply. 'I've told you what I intend, and I've sworn, by all that I hold dear, to see Antonio punished, exactly as it says in my bond. If you refuse to give me justice, people will say the laws of Venice are good for nothing, and your city's business life will suffer. You might ask me why I'd prefer a pound of useless flesh rather than three thousand ducats. Well, I'll tell you only that that is my wish, and that I hate Antonio!'

Bassanio could not stop himself jumping to his feet and shouting angrily, 'That's no answer, you unfeeling man! How can you be so cruel?'

'I don't have to please *you* with my answers,' Shylock said.

'But who kills a man just because he does not like him?' cried Bassanio desperately.

'Bassanio,' said Antonio in a tired voice, 'save your breath. There's no point in reasoning with him. You might as well ask the ocean to change its tides, or tell a wolf not to kill sheep. He has a heart of stone, and you'll never soften it. So please, let's get this finished. Let Shylock have what he wants.'

But Bassanio was insistent. 'Shylock, I'm offering you six thousand ducats instead of the three you lent us,' he said.

Shylock laughed in his face. 'If you were offering me thirty-six thousand ducats, I wouldn't take it! I want punishment! I claim justice!'

The Duke held up his hand for silence, and he turned to the money-lender, frowning. 'How can you hope for mercy from other people, if you offer none yourself?'

'I don't need to ask for mercy because I do no wrong!' replied Shylock. 'I paid for that pound of flesh which I now demand from Antonio. Will I get my judgement?'

The Duke looked concerned, and turned to one of his court officials. 'Has the lawyer, Doctor Bellario, arrived from Padua yet? I sent for him to help us reach a decision.'

The official stepped forward. 'A messenger has arrived with a letter from Doctor Bellario.'

'Ah, bring the messenger in, will you?' said the Duke.

'Don't worry, Antonio!' Bassanio called across the room to the merchant. 'Shylock shall have my flesh, blood, bones, and all, before I'll let you lose one drop of blood for me.'

Antonio simply shook his head. 'The weakest fruit drops earliest to the ground, Bassanio, and my time has come. I am ready for death.'

The court official brought in a young lawyer's clerk. There was a fresh, boyish look about him, and no one would have guessed that his face was really that of a woman, and that long hair was piled inside his hat. Even Gratiano did not recognize his new wife.

'Welcome to Venice, young man,' said the Duke with a smile. 'You come from Padua, from Doctor Bellario?'

Even Gratiano did not recognize his new wife.

'I do. The Doctor greets you and sends you this.' Nerissa handed a letter up to the Duke.

Meanwhile, Shylock had taken a large knife out of his coat pocket, and was sharpening it on the leather of his shoe.

Bassanio stared at him, horrified. 'What are you doing that for?' he asked the money-lender.

'To cut the flesh from that enemy of mine over there,' replied Shylock with an evil laugh. He smiled lovingly at the knife, which was catching the light from the window.

The Duke had not heard this. He looked up from the letter, saying, 'The good Bellario has sent us a lawyer – a young man he highly recommends. Where is this lawyer?'

'He's waiting outside this room,' said Nerissa, 'to know whether you'll give him permission to enter.'

'I will most gladly,' replied the Duke, adding to his officials, 'Go, bring in the young lawyer.'

He turned back to the court. 'While we're waiting, I'll read you Bellario's letter. He says:

> *"Unfortunately I am too sick to attend your court in Venice, as you request. But when your messenger arrived at my home, a young lawyer from Rome was visiting me. His name is Balthazar. I told him about the breaking of the bond that you described, and we discussed the case in detail. I have given him my opinion, and he comes to you, with his own excellent understanding of the law, to take my place. Don't let his age deceive you – he is indeed young, but I have never met a young man with such a wise head. Please accept him as my replacement." '*

A court official brought in Portia, dressed as a lawyer, all in black. Her long golden hair was hidden by a black hat, and she looked just like a beardless young man.

'And here he is,' said the Duke. 'Give me your hand, Balthazar, sir. You are very welcome here. Do you know all the facts of this case?'

'I have all the information I need,' answered Portia in her deepest voice. 'Who is the money-lender here, and who is the merchant?'

'Here is Shylock, the money-lender,' said the Duke, pointing to the old man.

'Your purpose seems a strange one,' Portia said to Shylock, 'but if you insist on punishment, the laws of Venice cannot stop you from taking it.' Turning back to the Duke, she said, 'And the merchant?'

'Here he is,' the Duke replied, pointing to Antonio.

'Do you accept that you signed the bond?' Portia asked him.

'Yes, I signed it,' answered Antonio with a sigh.

'Then the money-lender must be merciful,' said Portia.

'Why must I?' asked Shylock, frowning. 'Tell me that!'

'Mercy cannot be forced. It must be freely given,' she replied. 'It falls like gentle rain upon the ground below. It fills two hearts: the heart of the person who shows it and the heart of the person who receives it. Kings and princes can only be great men if they show mercy. Therefore, Shylock, though you ask for justice, consider this. If justice is applied to all of us, none of us will escape punishment. We beg for mercy, and that should teach us that we, in turn, should show mercy to others. Justice must go hand in hand with mercy, and I hope I have persuaded you of that. But, if you insist on your bond, this court must allow the merchant to be punished.'

'Let me be the judge of my own actions!' cried Shylock excitedly. 'I must have justice!'

Portia looked around the court and asked, 'Is the merchant able to repay the debt?'

Bassanio stepped eagerly forward to speak to the young lawyer. 'Yes, I have the money here. I can pay the debt twice or three times over! If this isn't enough, I'll sign a bond to pay it ten times over, and offer to lose my hands, my head, my heart if I can't find the money. If that isn't enough, it proves that Shylock just wants to destroy Antonio. I beg you, sir,' he said, turning to the Duke. 'Make the laws work for us! Do a little wrong in order to make something right, and prevent this evil man from succeeding in his plan.'

Portia shook her head, keeping her face turned away from Bassanio. 'We cannot go against the laws of Venice. If the bond is correctly written, and the bond is broken, then the punishment must take place. That's what the law says. And if we go against the law in this case, people in future cases will feel that they can follow this example.'

Shylock clapped his hands delightedly. 'Oh, what a wise young judge! Oh, thank you, wise young judge!'

'Kindly let me see the bond,' said Portia in a businesslike manner. Shylock handed it to her, and she examined it, and handed it back. 'Well, Shylock may lawfully claim a pound of flesh, which should be cut off by him nearest the merchant's heart. Be merciful, Shylock. Take three times the money and let me tear the bond in pieces.'

'Tear the bond in pieces when it's been paid!' replied Shylock, his eyes bright with excitement. 'You're an excellent judge and you know the law. So I call on you, give judgement. Nothing and nobody can change my intention.'

Antonio would have fallen if he had not been holding on to the back of a chair. 'These long arguments are too much for me,' he said weakly. 'I beg the court to give judgement.'

Portia sighed. 'Well then, here it is. Unbutton your shirt, Antonio, and prepare your chest for the knife—'

'Oh, noble judge! Oh, excellent young man!' cried Shylock, dancing about in delight, his knife in his hand.

'Because punishment is clearly needed if the bond is broken,' continued Portia.

'That's very true! Oh, wise judge!' cried Shylock. 'Yes, Antonio, your chest! That's what the bond says, doesn't it, judge? "Nearest his heart", those are the words, aren't they?'

'That's correct,' agreed Portia. 'Have you got scales here, Shylock, to weigh his flesh?'

'Yes, I have them ready,' replied Shylock eagerly.

Portia turned from him to Antonio. 'Merchant,' she said, 'have you anything to say?'

'Only a few words,' replied Antonio. 'I'm well prepared for death. Give me your hand, Bassanio. Good luck to you! Don't be sad for me. I think I'm fortunate – I won't live to be old and poor and miserable. Give my best wishes to your wife, and tell her how I died and how much I loved you. You may be sorry to lose a friend, but I'm not sorry to pay your debt. And if old Shylock cuts deep enough, I'll pay it at once, with all my heart.'

'Antonio,' said Bassanio, with tears in his eyes, 'I'm married to a wife who's as dear to me as life itself. But life itself, my wife, and all the world, are not as important to me as *your* life. I'd give all of them away if that would save you.'

Portia looked surprised and a little annoyed.

'If your wife were present to hear you make that offer,' she said sharply to Bassanio, 'she wouldn't thank you for it.'

Gratiano was also deeply moved, and stepped forward to

say, 'I too have a wife who I love dearly. But I would risk losing her if that would save Antonio!'

'It's lucky she can't hear you saying that,' Nerissa said, frowning, 'or there'd be raised voices in your house!'

Shylock was getting impatient. 'Come, come,' he said, 'time is passing. To the judgement, I beg you!'

'Shylock,' said Portia, taking a deep breath, 'a pound of the merchant's flesh is yours, according to the law and this court.'

'Most intelligent judge!' cried Shylock. 'Are you ready, Antonio? I have the knife here, and it's good and sharp—'

'But there is one thing,' said Portia, raising her hand. 'The bond does not allow you to take any blood at all. So if, in cutting, you make one drop of blood fall, under the laws of Venice you'll lose everything you own as a punishment.'

There was a sudden silence in the courtroom, and then Gratiano jumped to his feet in delight. 'Oh, wise judge!' he cried. 'Did you hear that, Shylock?'

For a moment, Shylock could not speak. His mouth opened, but no words came out. 'Is that the law?' he whispered at last.

Portia smiled confidently. 'It is. I can show you if you wish,' she said, holding up some papers. 'You asked for justice; this court now gives you the justice you demanded.'

Gratiano burst out laughing. 'Oh, noble judge! You were right, Shylock: he is a very wise judge!'

CHAPTER 13

Balthazar's Gift

🏵

Antonio, gratify this gentleman,
For in my mind you are much bound to him.

Shylock's shoulders were bent, and his head hung low. There was silence for a moment as he looked around the courtroom; his eyes were narrowed. 'I'll take the offer that was made to me, then,' he said at last. 'I'll accept three times the money, and let the merchant go.'

'Here's the money!' said Bassanio eagerly.

'No,' said Portia, shaking her head. 'He has refused it in open court. He shall have justice and the punishment laid out in his bond, and nothing more.'

'You mean I won't even get my three thousand ducats back?' asked Shylock miserably.

'You shall have nothing but the pound of flesh,' said Portia, 'and it shall be taken at your own risk, Shylock.'

The old man threw up his hands angrily. 'Well then, he can keep his flesh, and long may he enjoy it! I won't stay here any longer to be attacked like this!' He picked up his stick and was about to leave the courtroom, but Portia made a sign to a court official, who stood in front of the door to prevent his departure.

'The law has another hold on you, Shylock,' she said. 'One of the laws of Venice says that if someone attempts to take a person's life, one half of his wealth must go to the person he has threatened, and the other half to the city of Venice. The offender's life then depends on the Duke's mercy. You've tried to take Antonio's life, and broken this law. So beg the Duke for mercy!'

The Duke rose from the judge's chair. 'Shylock,' he said, 'I want you to see the difference between us. You refused to be merciful to Antonio, but I will show you mercy before you even ask for it. I won't have you put to death, but one half of your wealth will go to Antonio. The other half should be given to the city of Venice, but we may be generous and take only part of it.'

'Take my life as well!' sobbed Shylock, tears rolling down his ancient face. 'You might as well take everything if you take all my money. I'm a money-lender – what can I do, without my money?'

Portia turned to Antonio. 'What mercy can you show him, Antonio?' she asked.

Antonio was having difficulty understanding that he was not about to die. But he straightened up and began to speak, hesitantly at first. 'Well… if the Duke agrees, I suggest that Shylock keeps one half of his wealth, as long as he'll let me take care of the other half.' He passed a hand over his face, then continued, more clearly. 'I'll keep it safe and, on Shylock's death, I'll give it to his daughter's husband, Lorenzo. Also, I would ask for Shylock to make a will, giving everything he owns to his daughter Jessica and her husband when he dies.'

The Duke nodded. 'Shylock, you will do this, or else I will change the court's judgement and show you no mercy.'

There was silence for a moment.

'Do you agree, Shylock?' asked Portia.

'I do,' whispered Shylock in a trembling voice. 'Now please let me leave this court. I'm not well. Send any papers you like to my house and I'll sign them.'

'You may leave,' said the Duke. 'Balthazar's clerk will deliver the papers to you. Sign them and return them at once.'

The court official stepped away from the door, and Shylock walked slowly out, his stick tapping on the wooden floor.

The Duke turned to Portia. 'Sir, I beg you to have dinner with me tonight.'

'Please accept my apologies,' replied Portia with a smile, 'but unfortunately I need to leave at once.'

'What a pity!' said the Duke. 'Antonio, you are much in this gentleman's debt – you must show him how grateful you are. Goodbye, gentlemen!' He stepped down from the platform, and everyone in the room stood up as he left.

Bassanio and Gratiano rushed over to congratulate Antonio, and Bassanio shook Portia's hand warmly. 'Noble sir,' he said, deeply moved, 'your wise words today have saved my friend from a terrible punishment. Please accept from us the money that we owed the money-lender.'

'And we'll still be in your debt for ever,' added Antonio.

'I'm happy with the result of the trial,' replied Portia, 'and that is payment enough for me, so please keep your ducats. I hope you'll remember me when we meet again. Good day to you.' She turned to leave, but Bassanio held her back.

'Dear sir, I cannot let you go empty-handed,' he said. 'If you won't accept money, please take something from us, not in payment, but as a small gift to show how grateful we are.'

Portia hesitated. 'As you insist, I *will* take something. Give me the ring on your finger – I'll take that to remember you.'

Bassanio looked shocked. 'This ring, good sir? Oh, it's worth nothing. I'd be ashamed to give you this.'

'That's the only thing I want,' said Portia, a little crossly. 'And I really would like it.'

'I will take something. Give me the ring on your finger.'

'I'm so sorry, but this ring is precious to me,' cried Bassanio desperately. 'I'll find the most valuable ring in Venice and give it to you! But forgive me, not this ring!'

'I see, sir,' Portia replied coldly, 'that you're good at offering, but not so good at giving.'

'Good sir, this ring was given to me by my wife,' said Bassanio, 'and she made me swear never to lose it.'

'Huh!' said Portia, with a bitter laugh. 'That's what many men say to avoid making gifts! Unless your wife is mad, she'd realize how much I deserve this ring, and she wouldn't be angry. Well, goodbye!' And she and Nerissa left the courtroom.

Antonio took Bassanio's arm. 'I beg you, let the young man have the ring,' he said, with tears in his eyes. 'Think what he's done for us! Remember that he's saved my life!'

Bassanio could not refuse his friend. He took the ring off his finger and handed it to Gratiano. 'Go, Gratiano,' he said, 'run and catch up with the young lawyer. Give him this ring!'

Gratiano nodded and ran out of the room. Bassanio and Antonio walked out together slowly, both still finding it hard to believe that all danger was now past.

'Tomorrow morning, dear Antonio, we shall go to Belmont together,' said Bassanio.

Just around the corner, outside the palace, Portia was handing some papers to Nerissa. 'Ask where Shylock's house is,' she said, 'take these papers to him, and let him sign them. Then we can catch the next ferry to Belmont.'

'We'll be at home before our husbands!' replied Nerissa with a smile.

'Wait, young sirs!' They turned to see who was calling. It was Gratiano, hurrying to catch them up. 'Lord Bassanio has changed his mind, and sends you his ring,' he said breathlessly.

'I accept his ring most gratefully,' said Portia. 'And as you're here, would you show my clerk the way to Shylock's house?'

'I'd be delighted,' said Gratiano, smiling politely.

As he turned to lead the way, Nerissa whispered in her mistress's ear, 'Now I'll see if I can get my husband's ring, which I made him swear to keep for ever.'

Portia laughed quietly and whispered back, 'It'll be very amusing to hear what our husbands say when we ask where the rings are!'

CHAPTER 14

Back to Belmont

I gave my love a ring, and made him swear
Never to part with it, and here he stands.

It was past midnight, and Portia's garden in Belmont seemed an almost magical place in the moonlight. Lorenzo and Jessica were walking hand in hand down a grassy path.

'The moon shines so brightly!' Lorenzo remarked. 'It was on a night like this that beautiful Jessica escaped from her cruel father, the wealthy money-lender, and ran away to Belmont.'

Jessica smiled and held her husband's hand tightly. 'On a night like this, young Lorenzo swore he loved Jessica, and made her many promises, none of which he can possibly keep.'

'On a night like this, Jessica made terrible accusations about her husband, and he forgave her,' laughed Lorenzo.

'On a night like this… Listen, Lorenzo, I can hear footsteps!'

'Who comes here to Lady Portia's house in the middle of the night?' Lorenzo called out.

A man in servant's uniform was hurrying towards them. 'It is me – Stephano – sir,' he said, 'Lady Portia's servant. She's sent me with a message for you. She says she and her maid will arrive home before sunrise. Can you tell me, sir, has my master, Lord Bassanio, returned home yet?'

'Not yet,' replied Lorenzo. 'We're waiting for news.'

Just then, a loud shout was heard. 'Master Lorenzo! Master Lorenzo!' Another man was coming through the gate, and as he ran up to them they saw that it was Lancelot Gobbo. 'Ah, there you are, sir!' he cried breathlessly. 'Lord Bassanio has sent me on ahead to say he'll be here soon.'

'Stephano and Lancelot,' said Lorenzo, 'go indoors and tell the other servants to make preparations for Lady Portia and Lord Bassanio's arrival.'

The two servants nodded and went towards the house, while Lorenzo and Jessica sat down on a stone seat in the garden.

'Let's wait here for them, my sweet,' said Lorenzo, and before long, sitting in the moonlight and enjoying the warm night air, they both fell asleep.

They woke to the sound of voices quite close to them. 'Ah!' cried Lorenzo. 'Unless I'm very much mistaken, that's Portia's voice!' And, jumping up from his seat, he greeted Portia and Nerissa, who were walking along the path.

'We've been worrying about our husbands, Lorenzo,' Portia said. 'Have they returned yet?'

'Not yet, madam, but we've heard they're on their way.'

'I don't want the servants to say a word about our absence from home,' said Portia. 'And you, Lorenzo and Jessica, please don't mention it either.'

'We can keep your secret, madam!' replied Lorenzo. 'You've only just arrived in time. Look, here comes your husband now!'

A coach and horses had stopped on the road outside, and three gentlemen got out. Bassanio, who was first through the gate, hurried along the path to greet his wife, followed by Gratiano and Antonio.

'Sweet Portia, how I've missed you!' Bassanio said, taking her in his arms. 'Please welcome my friend. This is Antonio, to whom I owe so much.'

Antonio stepped forward and took Portia's hand. 'But I have been well repaid,' he said, smiling at Bassanio.

'Sir, you are very welcome in our house,' Portia told him.

But above her greeting, they now heard the sound of Gratiano's raised voice. He sounded upset. 'By the moon above, I swear you accuse me falsely! I tell you, I gave it to the lawyer's clerk! I can't see why you're so upset about it, my love.'

Portia turned to him, with a smile. 'An argument already, between you and Nerissa? What's the matter?'

Gratiano looked annoyed. 'Oh, it's about a gold ring, a cheap thing that she gave me, with some foolish words of love on it – "Love me and never leave me".'

'A cheap ring, was it? Foolish words of love, were they?' cried Nerissa angrily. 'You swore when I gave it to you to wear it until you died! You swore it would lie with you in your grave! Gave it to a lawyer's clerk, did you? You think I'm fool enough to believe that? You gave it to a woman – I know you did!'

'I swear to you,' Gratiano insisted, 'I gave it to the lawyer's clerk. He begged me for it as payment, and I couldn't refuse him.'

Portia looked very serious. 'I must speak plainly, Gratiano. You were to blame for giving away so lightly your wife's first gift to you – a ring you'd sworn to keep for ever. I myself gave my love a ring and made him swear never to part with it.' She smiled confidently and lovingly at Bassanio, whose face was getting paler by the minute. 'I can promise you that *he* would never give it away, for all the wealth in the world. I'm disappointed in you, Gratiano. You're making your poor wife most unhappy. If that happened to me, I'd be very angry.'

Bassanio did not know where to look. 'It might be better to cut my left hand off,' he whispered to Antonio, 'and pretend I lost the ring while fighting for it!'

Gratiano was unable to keep silent. 'Well, Bassanio gave *his* ring away to the lawyer who saved Antonio's life. And then the boy, his clerk, asked for *my* ring. Neither clerk nor lawyer would take any other payment, so what could we do?'

'What ring did you give the lawyer?' Portia asked in an icy voice. 'Not the one *I* gave you, I hope?'

Her husband had difficulty in meeting her eyes. 'Portia,' he said unhappily, 'I won't make my fault worse by lying to you. You see my finger has no ring on it. The ring is gone.'

'So your promises to me were false!' cried Portia angrily. 'Well, you're no longer my husband – not until I see that ring again.'

'Nor you mine!' said Nerissa to Gratiano.

'Sweet Portia,' begged Bassanio, his voice full of feeling, 'if you knew who asked for the ring, why I gave the ring, and how unwillingly I parted with the ring, you wouldn't be so angry with me. He would accept nothing but the ring!'

Portia replied sharply, 'I depended on you to keep that ring! If you'd given a thought to me, you'd never have parted with it. No one would have forced you to give them a ring that had such an important meaning. I think Nerissa is right – you and Gratiano each gave your ring to some woman!'

'No, by my honour,' cried Bassanio desperately, 'I gave it to a young lawyer, who saved the life of my dear friend here, and wouldn't take the three thousand ducats we offered him. I had no choice – he begged me for it, and was very displeased when I refused to give it to him. Forgive me, sweet lady!'

'All these arguments are my fault,' said Antonio miserably. '*I* was the one who begged Bassanio to give the ring to the lawyer – there seemed no other way of thanking him.'

'Please don't be concerned, sir,' said Portia. 'You are welcome here in spite of these disagreements.'

'Portia,' continued Bassanio, 'I swear to you, by everything that I hold most dear, that if you forgive me, I'll never break a promise to you again!'

'I once lent my life for your husband, madam,' Antonio said, 'and would have died if that lawyer hadn't helped me. But I will make another bond, on my own life, that Bassanio will never break his word to you again.'

'I accept your promise, Antonio,' said Portia, taking a ring off her finger, 'so give him this, and tell him to keep it better than the other one.'

'Here, Bassanio,' said Antonio, handing the ring to his friend, 'swear at once to keep this ring!'

'Goodness, how can this be? It's the same one I gave the young lawyer!' cried Bassanio in great surprise, as he took it.

Portia nodded. 'He gave it to me. You see, I know the young lawyer very well. You could say we are… very close.'

'And the boy, the lawyer's clerk,' added Nerissa, smiling, 'I know *him* very well! He gave me *my* ring. Here it is.'

The two husbands looked at each other in horror. So, while they had been away, their wives had been secretly visited by the two young men from Rome! How had they met these young men? And why had the men given them their rings? Bassanio and Gratiano were deeply shocked: they had been deceived.

'Wait till I find that clerk,' cried Gratiano jealously. 'I'll kill him, that's what I'll do!'

But Portia took pity on the two men. 'I think it's time to tell you what really happened,' she said with a smile. 'With help from my cousin Bellario, I disguised myself as the lawyer at Antonio's trial, and Nerissa was the clerk. Here's Bellario's letter – you can read it if you like. Lorenzo there will witness that we left Belmont the same time as you, and have only just returned.'

'Here, Bassanio,' said Antonio, 'swear at once to keep this ring!'

'So you never went to that quiet place you mentioned, madam?' said Lorenzo. 'You went to Venice instead!'

Bassanio could not believe it. 'Were you really the lawyer, and I didn't recognize you?' he asked.

'And were you the clerk who gave my ring to my wife?' Gratiano said, turning to Nerissa with a smile.

'Well, my dear young lawyer, whenever I'm away, I shall trust you to look after my wife!' laughed Bassanio.

'I have good news for Antonio, too,' said Portia. 'On our way home, we heard that three of your ships have arrived safely in harbour.'

'Sweet lady,' replied Antonio gratefully, 'that is wonderful news! You have given me back my life, and now you bring me great fortune.'

'And Lorenzo,' added Portia, 'Nerissa has something which will please you, too. It is a copy of Shylock's signed will, in which he leaves all his wealth to you and your wife Jessica when he dies.'

'Ladies,' replied Lorenzo, 'you have brought good news for everybody.'

Portia looked up at the sky. 'Look, it's almost morning. I think we should go indoors now – I'm sure you will all want to hear more about our time in Venice.' Taking Bassanio's hand, she added, 'I think we'll be happy in the future, don't you?'

Her husband kissed her hand. 'I'm sure we will!' he replied.

'And so will we!' cried Gratiano. 'But as long as I live, I'll fear nothing so much as losing Nerissa's ring!'

The three couples, with Antonio, walked slowly along the path towards the house, laughing and talking together. And soon the garden was quiet again in the pale light of early morning.

The Merchant of Venice

PLAYSCRIPTS

I hold the world but as the world, Gratiano:
A stage, where every man must play a part...

PLAY 1: A LETTER FROM VENICE

Characters in this play

Portia a lady of Belmont
Bassanio a young man from Venice
Gratiano ⎫
Salarino ⎬ Bassanio's friends
Lorenzo ⎭
Jessica Lorenzo's wife

Background

In the contest of the caskets, Bassanio has just made the correct choice, and he and Portia are now engaged to be married. Gratiano has also become engaged to Nerissa, so as this scene begins, the four young people are very happy. However, Bassanio is about to receive some very bad news.

Notes

This scene takes place in Belmont, in Portia's study.
This play is for six actors.

You will need:

• a letter for Salarino to deliver to Bassanio

PLAYSCRIPT 1

At Portia's house in Belmont.

Portia, Bassanio, and Gratiano are all standing in the study; they are laughing and talking together. The door opens, and Lorenzo, Jessica, and Salarino enter the room.

BASSANIO *(in great surprise)* My dear friends! What a wonderful surprise! Welcome to Belmont! *(turning to Portia)* These are two friends of mine from Venice, Lorenzo and Salarino, and this is Lorenzo's young wife Jessica.

Lorenzo, Salarino, and Jessica greet Portia; then they greet Gratiano (who they know already).

PORTIA *(smiling)* As friends of yours, they're very welcome.

LORENZO Thank you, my lady, but *(turning to Bassanio)* I fear you may not be so happy, Bassanio, when you hear the reason for our visit. Jessica and I weren't planning to disturb you here, but by chance we met Salarino, who was on his way here from Venice with an important letter for you. You must read it at once. It's from Antonio.

GRATIANO Ah, good Antonio! What a fine man he is! I know he'll be glad to hear our good news.

SALARINO *(looking serious)* I think he'd be glad to have a little good news himself.

Salarino steps forward and hands the letter to Bassanio, who opens it at once. He looks shocked as he reads and re-reads Antonio's letter. Portia watches him anxiously.

PORTIA *(whispering to herself)* See how pale he is! Has some dear friend of his died? What else could it be? *(speaking aloud to Bassanio)* Bassanio, tell me the worst. I want to share the troubles this letter brings you.

BASSANIO *(looking at Portia with his face full of pain)* My lady, when I first spoke to you of love, I explained that I had no wealth, that I was a gentleman, nothing more. I should have told you that I had less than nothing, because in fact, I'm deep in debt, to my dearest, closest friend, who borrowed money from his bitterest enemy to help me. And now this letter tells me that my friend is in terrible danger.

(turning to Salarino) But Salarino, is it true? Have *all* his ships sunk?

SALARINO *(nodding his head sadly)* Not a single ship has arrived home safely, so Antonio doesn't have enough money to repay the bond. But Shylock would now refuse to take the money anyway. I've never known a man so determined to destroy someone. He has told the Duke again and again that he must have justice.

JESSICA *(coming forward and looking worriedly at Bassanio)* My father has always hated Antonio. And I know that he will make things very difficult for him.

PORTIA *(to Bassanio)* How much does your friend Antonio owe this money-lender?

BASSANIO *(miserably)* Three thousand ducats – that's what he borrowed for me.

PORTIA *(laughing)* Is that all? Pay him six thousand, and
destroy the bond! Double six thousand, and then three
times that figure, before such a dear friend shall lose a hair
through your fault. First, we'll get married, and then you'll
go to Venice, with gold to pay this miserable debt. Come,
my love, this is your wedding day! Give your friends a
proper welcome, and try to be cheerful.

*Bassanio puts his head in his hands, and Portia, looking at him,
speaks more softly.*

PORTIA Let me hear your friend's letter.

BASSANIO *(starts reading Antonio's letter aloud)* 'My friend
Bassanio, my ships have all sunk, and I was not able to
repay Shylock in time. And since, in paying the bond, it
is impossible for me to live, all debts are cleared between
you and me. I ask only that I might be able to see you at
my death. But please decide this for yourself. Come only if
your feelings for me as a friend persuade you to – and not
because of this letter.'

As he finishes reading the letter, Portia is crying.

PORTIA Now I understand why you're so miserable! Please,
get through all your business here and go at once!

BASSANIO Since you are happy for me to go away, my sweet,
I will hurry to Antonio as soon as we have been married.
But be in no doubt, I shall not sleep until I am back at your
side.
  (turning to Gratiano) Come, Gratiano, there's no time to
lose.

Gratiano and Bassanio hurry out. Lorenzo and Jessica look anxiously at each other. Portia sits down, with a hand to her head. Salarino remains standing, looking concerned.

PLAY 2: THE RING

Characters in this play

Antonio a merchant of Venice
Bassanio Antonio's friend
Gratiano a friend of Antonio and Bassanio
Portia a young lady of Belmont, disguised as a lawyer
Nerissa Portia's maid, disguised as a lawyer's clerk

Background

These two scenes take place at the end of Antonio's trial. Portia, in her lawyer's disguise, has shown that Shylock was at fault and must be punished. She has saved Antonio's life, so he and his friend Bassanio are very grateful to her. But Portia and Nerissa look so much like two young men that even their husbands, Bassanio and Gratiano, do not recognize them, and because of this, Portia and Nerissa intend to play an amusing trick on their husbands.

Notes

Scene 1 takes place in the courtroom.
Scene 2 takes place in the street outside the court. This can be in a different corner of the classroom.
This play is for five actors.

You will need:
- a chair for the judge's seat
- black coats and hats for Portia and Nerissa
- papers for Portia to hold
- a ring (on Bassanio's finger in Scene 1, and in Gratiano's hand in Scene 2)

PLAYSCRIPT 2

Scene 1

In the courtroom at the Duke's palace in Venice. The Duke has given judgement, Shylock has left the court, and the Duke and his officials have also just left. Only Bassanio, Antonio, Gratiano, Portia, and Nerissa are still in the room. Bassanio rushes over to Portia and shakes her hand warmly.

BASSANIO *(deeply moved)* Noble sir, your wise words today have saved my friend from a terrible punishment. Please accept from us the money that we owed the money-lender.

ANTONIO *(to Portia)* And we'll still be in your debt for ever.

PORTIA I'm happy with the result of the trial, and that is payment enough for me, so please keep your ducats. I hope you'll remember me when we meet again. Good day to you.

Portia turns to go, with Nerissa, but Bassanio holds her back.

BASSANIO Dear sir, if you won't accept money, please take something from us, not in payment, but as a small gift to show how grateful we are.

PORTIA *(hesitating for a moment)* As you insist, I *will* take something. Give me the ring on your finger – I'll take that to remember you.

BASSANIO *(looking shocked and holding up his ring finger)* This ring, good sir? Oh, it's worth nothing. I'd be ashamed to give you this.

PORTIA *(a little crossly)* That's the only thing I want. And I really would like it.

BASSANIO *(desperately)* I'm so sorry, but this ring is precious to me. I'll find the most valuable ring in Venice and give it to you! But forgive me, not this ring!

PORTIA *(coldly)* I see, sir, that you're good at offering, but not so good at giving.

BASSANIO Good sir, this ring was given to me by my wife, and she made me swear never to lose it.

PORTIA *(with a bitter laugh)* Huh! That's what many men say to avoid making gifts! Unless your wife is mad, she'd realize how much I deserve this ring, and she wouldn't be angry. Well, goodbye!

Portia and Nerissa leave the courtroom.

ANTONIO *(very upset, taking Bassanio's arm)* I beg you, let the young man have the ring. Think what he's done for us! Remember that he's saved my life!

Bassanio unwillingly takes the ring off his finger.

BASSANIO *(turning to Gratiano and giving the ring to him)* Go, Gratiano, run and catch up with the young lawyer. Give him this ring!

Gratiano nods and runs out of the room. Bassanio and Antonio walk out together more slowly, talking quietly.

Scene 2

In the street outside the court, a few minutes later.

Portia and Nerissa, still disguised as lawyer and clerk, are talking to each other. Portia hands some papers to Nerissa.

PORTIA *(to Nerissa)* Ask where Shylock's house is. Take these papers to him, and let him sign them. Then we can catch the next ferry to Belmont.

NERISSA *(with a smile)* We'll be at home before our husbands!

Gratiano enters, hurrying to catch them up. Portia and Nerissa hear him coming and they turn to see who it is.

GRATIANO *(breathlessly)* Wait, young sirs! Lord Bassanio has changed his mind, and sends you his ring.

Gratiano holds out Bassanio's ring.

PORTIA I accept his ring most gratefully. *(She takes the ring and puts it on her finger.)* And as you're here, would you show my clerk the way to Shylock's house?

GRATIANO *(smiling politely)* I'd be delighted.

Gratiano starts to walk away.

NERISSA *(turning to Portia and whispering in her mistress's ear with a smile)* Now I'll see if I can get my husband's ring, which I made him swear to keep for ever.

PORTIA *(laughing quietly and whispering back to Nerissa)*
It'll be very amusing to hear what our husbands say when
we ask where the rings are! Off you go with Gratiano, and
be quick. I'll be waiting for you at the harbour.

*Portia watches with a smile as Gratiano walks away with
Nerissa. He is talking pleasantly to her, thinking that she is the
young lawyer's clerk.*

GLOSSARY

bond *(n)* an important legal agreement; a paper containing this agreement

breed *(v)* to cause something (past tense **bred**)

casket *(n)* a small box for holding jewels, etc.

claim *(v)* to ask for something because it is yours

clerk *(n)* a person whose job is to do written work

contest *(n)* a game or competition that people try to win

court *(n)* the place where a person is judged on whether they have done something wrong, and what the punishment will be

debt *(n)* money that you must pay back to someone

deceive *(v)* to deliberately make somebody believe something that is not true

deserve *(v)* to be good or bad enough to have something

desire *(v)* to feel that you want something very much

disguise *(n & v)* to change the appearance of somebody or something so that people will not know who or what they are

Duke *(n)* one of the most important men in a country

evil *(adj)* bad and cruel

flesh *(n)* the soft part of your body under your skin

gain *(n & v)* to get something that you want or need

gentleman *(n)* a man of a high position in society

glitter *(v)* to shine brightly with a lot of small flashes of light

goods *(n)* things that you buy or sell

hazard *(v)* to risk (old-fashioned)

honour *(n)* something that makes you proud and pleased

honourable *(adj)* behaving in a way that makes you respected

interest *(n)* the extra money that you pay back if you borrow money, or that you receive if you put money in a bank

justice *(n)* being fair to people; the law

lady *(n)* a name used when talking to women who have an important position in society

lead *(n)* a soft grey metal that is very heavy

lord *(n)* a name used when talking to people like dukes

loss *(n)* losing something

maid *(n)* a woman servant who works in another person's house

mask *(n)* a thing over your face that hides or protects it

master *(n)* a man who controls others (people or animals)

merchant *(n)* a person whose job is to travel around the world, buying and selling many goods

merciful *(adj)* feeling or showing mercy

mercy *(n)* kindness and forgiveness shown to someone who has done wrong

mistress *(n)* a woman who controls others (people or animals)

noble *(adj)* good, honest, and caring about other people; important in society

nod *(v)* to move your head down and up again quickly, usually because you agree with or understand something

pound *(n)* a measure of weight (= 0.454 kilograms)

prince *(n)* a man in a royal family, especially the son of a king or queen

relief *(n)* the good feeling you have when pain or worry stops

rule *(n)* something that tells you what you must or mustn't do

scales *(n)* a machine that shows how heavy people or things are

sigh *(v)* to let out a deep breath, e.g. because you are sad

Signor *(n)* the Italian word for Mr

skill *(n)* the ability to do something well

skull *(n)* the bones in the head of a person or an animal

sob *(v)* to cry loudly, making short sounds

spit *(v)*   to send liquid or food out from your mouth (past tense **spat**)

suitor *(n)*   a man who wants to marry a particular woman

swear *(v)*   to make a serious promise (past tense **swore**)

trust *(v)*   to believe that somebody is honest and good

will *(n)*   a piece of paper that says who will have your money, house, etc. when you die

STORY NOTES

Belmont Portia's home, a fictional place created by Shakespeare

Count Palatine an important nobleman who governed for a king in a particular area

ducats coins that were used for trade in Europe in later medieval times

Genoa a Mediterranean city which was a republic (a country with no king or queen, in which the government is chosen by the people) in the sixteenth century, and home to many famous artists

Grand Canal one of the most important canals in Venice

Latin the language of Ancient Rome

Naples a city in southern Italy which was governed by Spain in the sixteenth century

Padua a city in northern Italy which was governed by Venice in the sixteenth century

Piazza San Marco Venice's main square, which dates back to the twelfth century, and has long been the centre of Venetian life

Rialto a busy shopping area in the heart of Venice today; but in the sixteenth century, the city's business centre, with banks and markets, where people met to hear the city's news

Rialto Bridge a covered stone footbridge, one of the four bridges over the Grand Canal; it was built between 1588 and 1591, and there are shops and restaurants on it

ABOUT SIXTEENTH-CENTURY VENICE

Venice is a city in north-eastern Italy, built on a group of small islands separated by canals and joined by bridges.

In the early sixteenth century, it was the second largest city in Europe, and one of the richest in the world. It had become famous as a fashionable city where many foreigners came to live and work, and where a lot of great art and writing was produced.

Venice was wealthy because it was a very important centre for trade – taking goods like silks, gold, jewellery, and similarly expensive things from Italy and other countries across the world in sailing ships for people to buy; and then bringing

other things back to sell at home. There were therefore many rich merchants in Venice, and the city was one of the first in Europe to have proper banks and money-lending and borrowing businesses.

At this time, Venice was governed as an independent republic by its Duke and by an important group called the Council of Ten. Because of its wealth, the republic controlled many areas around the Adriatic Sea.

These days, Venice is considered by many people to be the most beautiful city in the world. Tourism provides most of its income, and its museums and palaces are known throughout the world.

IDEAS IN THIS STORY

Money

One of the main themes in this story is money, and the effect it has on people. Antonio, as a merchant, works with money every day, and so does Shylock, as a money-lender. But while Shylock is greedy, and charges interest on the money people borrow from him, Antonio lends his money for free, and gives generously to Bassanio so that he can compete with Portia's much richer suitors.

The effect greed has on people was clearly a concern for Portia's father. His daughter was wealthy, and he must have realized that many people would want to marry her for her money, so he insisted on the contest of the caskets.

Money is in Jessica's mind, too, when she runs away to marry Lorenzo. She takes not only her mother's jewels, but also two large bags of ducats; she knows that this money will make married life easier for her and Lorenzo. It is the loss of this money and his jewels, more than the loss of his daughter, that upsets Shylock.

Opposites

There is greed and generosity in this story, and there are other opposites too, like love and hate. Antonio and Bassanio love each other as true friends and companions, and three young couples fall in love and marry; but Shylock hates Antonio and his friends with the greatest bitterness.

We also see mercy and revenge in this story: the Duke, the court, and Antonio are all ready to be merciful to Shylock, but Shylock insists on trying to take his revenge.

Even the two places in the story, Venice and Belmont, are the opposite of each other. Venice is a very wealthy city, with merchants bringing goods in and out every day, and it is a city controlled by men. Belmont, on the other hand, is a gentle place for love and fun, and here women are in charge.

The contest of the caskets

The contest of the caskets is an interesting puzzle for Portia's suitors to solve. The correct casket is the one made of the dullest metal, lead; this is the one chosen by Bassanio, with a little help from the song Portia's musicians play. Shakespeare seems to be saying that something which looks valuable may not contain anything precious, and that outward appearances can mislead people. This was perhaps an unusual idea in sixteenth-century Venice, where gold or silver would always be preferable to a cheaper, plainer metal like lead.

The rings

The rings have two purposes in the story. Firstly, they show Portia's cleverness in tricking Bassanio and Gratiano, and in making them swear everlasting love to their wives again. Secondly, as Bassanio and Gratiano give the rings to friends (the lawyer and his clerk) who are also their wives, perhaps Shakespeare wanted us to think that there would be friendship as well as love in these two marriages.

ABOUT WILLIAM SHAKESPEARE

William Shakespeare (1564–1616) was born in Stratford-upon-Avon, a small town in central England. His father was a glove-maker and wool merchant, and his mother, Mary Arden, was the daughter of a landowner.

Little is known about Shakespeare's early life. He went to school in Stratford, and at eighteen he married a local girl called Anne Hathaway, with whom he had three children. His wife and children stayed in Stratford, but by 1592, Shakespeare was living in London, writing plays and also working as an actor. In 1594, he joined a company of actors called The Lord Chamberlain's Men, and began to write more and more plays: he produced about two a year until 1611.

In 1595, Shakespeare wrote *Romeo and Juliet*, his famous play about love and families at war. In 1599, The Lord Chamberlain's Men built a theatre called The Globe, where many of Shakespeare's plays were performed. The company also acted the plays before Queen Elizabeth I and then King James I. In King James I's time, the Lord Chamberlain's Men were renamed the King's Men.

By the time he was in his late forties, Shakespeare was successful and rich, buying houses and land in London and Stratford. He died in Stratford on his birthday in 1616, when he was only fifty-two years old.

Today, you can visit his homes in the town, and there is also an important theatre company there called the Royal Shakespeare Company, which gives performances of his works and other productions. You can read more about the events and people in Shakespeare's life in a story in the Oxford Bookworms Library, *William Shakespeare* (at Stage 2).

Shakespeare wrote thirty-seven plays, and more than 150 sonnets (fourteen-line poems) – and *The Merchant of Venice*, which was written between 1596 and 1598, was one of his earlier works. The first known performance of the play was by the King's Men in 1605 at the court of King James I, but it had probably been performed before then.

Since then, there have been films, operas, and many theatre productions of *The Merchant of Venice*. One of the biggest questions for directors and actors, when they perform this play, is how to show Shylock's character. He seems to be a cruel, greedy old man, and in the past, this is how he normally appeared in productions. However, in more modern performances, Shylock is often shown as a sympathetic character who people should pity. After all, the other characters in the play accuse him of dishonesty – but they are happy to trick him in order to defeat him.

In Shylock, Shakespeare created a complicated character that audiences around the world continue to discuss today, and this is one of the reasons why *The Merchant of Venice* remains such an interesting and popular play.

The Merchant of Venice

ACTIVITIES

ACTIVITIES

Before Reading

1 **Match the words below to the definitions.**

casket   contest   debt   justice   merchant   pound

1 a small box for holding jewels, etc.
2 money that you must pay back to someone
3 a person whose job is to buy and sell goods
4 a game or competition that people try to win
5 a measure of weight
6 being fair to people

2 **What do you know about William Shakespeare and the plays he wrote? Are these sentences true or false?**

William Shakespeare…
1 lived most of his life in Scotland.
2 was an actor and a writer.
3 travelled widely in Europe.
4 wrote *Hamlet* and *Othello*.
5 wrote *Everyman* and *My Fair Lady*.

3 **Look at the front and back cover, and the chapter titles. Choose the correct word or phrase to complete the sentences.**

The story…
1 takes place in the *15th / 16th* century.
2 is set in the beautiful city of *Paris / Venice*.
3 is about a *lady / gentleman* who owes money.
4 includes several characters *at war / in love*.
5 provides a *happy / sad* ending for most characters.

ACTIVITIES

While Reading

Read Chapter 1. Match the quotes to the people who say them in the story.

Antonio   Bassanio   Gratiano   Salarino   Solanio

1 'A merchant's life is full of worry; we all understand that.'
2 'Well then, let's just say the reason you're sad is that you're not happy, and leave it at that!'
3 'It's much better to play the fool and have a face lined from laughter than to let your heart turn cold from sadness.'
4 'If I had the money to compete with them, I feel sure I could win her love!'
5 'Just say what you want me to do and I'll do it!'

Read Chapter 2. Match the sentence halves.

1 In order to find the best husband for Portia, …
2 There are three caskets…
3 If a suitor fails to choose correctly, …
4 Portia does not like any of the gentlemen…
5 Nerissa cheers Portia up…

a he has to leave Belmont at once.
b her father created a contest.
c by telling her the five noblemen are leaving.
d which Portia's suitors must choose from.
e who have asked for her hand in marriage.

Read Chapter 3. Are these sentences true or false?

1 Shylock pretends to be less clever than he really is.
2 Antonio needs money to pay his debt to Bassanio.
3 Shylock enjoys making Bassanio ask again and again for the money.
4 Shylock has hated Antonio for a long time.
5 Shylock has three thousand ducats at his house.
6 The punishment for breaking the bond is a pound of flesh.
7 Antonio agrees that he will sign Shylock's bond.
8 Antonio is worried that he will not be able to repay Shylock in time.

Read Chapter 4. Choose the correct words to complete the sentences.

1 The Prince says he is famous for his *intelligence / bravery*.
2 There are three *promises / plans* that all suitors must make.
3 The three caskets are kept behind a *wall / curtain*.
4 The Prince chooses the *silver / gold* casket.
5 There is a *skull / jewel* inside the casket.
6 Portia is *disappointed / relieved* to see the Prince depart.

Read Chapter 5. Correct the underlined words in each sentence to make the sentences true.

1 Lancelot Gobbo delivers Jessica's present to Lorenzo.
2 Shylock gives his moneybags to Jessica.
3 Jessica disguises herself as a neighbour's boy.
4 Shylock and Salarino help Lorenzo.
5 Jessica takes her grandmother's jewellery with her.
6 Lorenzo and Jessica plan to stay in Venice.

Read Chapter 6. Put the events in order.

a The Duke of Venice arrives with his soldiers.

b Bassanio's ship sails away from Venice.

c Shylock rushes into the harbour, shouting wildly.

d Antonio says goodbye to Bassanio.

e Shylock is carried back home by the Duke's soldiers.

f Antonio explains that Jessica and Lorenzo left earlier.

Read Chapter 7. Are these sentences true or false?

1 Portia is pleased to see the Prince of Aragon.

2 Only one casket contains Portia's picture.

3 The Prince likes to do the same as other men.

4 There is a picture of a ghost in the casket he chooses.

5 The result of the contest makes the Prince very angry.

6 A relation of Nerissa's arrives at Belmont.

Read Chapter 8. Then complete the sentences with the names. Some of the names are used more than once.

Antonio   Jessica   Salarino   Shylock   Solanio   Tubal

1 At the beginning of the chapter, ... reports bad news to his friend ... about a ship belonging to ... .

2 The two friends are shocked to hear ... talk about his plans for revenge.

3 ... had sent his friend ... to search for ... in Genoa.

4 ... is more upset about losing his money and jewels than losing his daughter ... .

5 People in Venice are saying that ... is a ruined man, and ... is delighted to hear it.

6 ... is determined to claim his pound of flesh from ... .

Read Chapter 9. Who says these things? Read the quotes and write the name of the speaker.

1 'A girl has to be careful who she trusts.'
2 'I promise I'll love you until my dying day!'
3 'I *may* accept you, sir.'
4 'I am all yours, whatever fortune may decide!'
5 'How often the world is deceived by outward show!'
6 'I wonder if that's a clue.'

Read Chapter 10. Correct the <u>underlined</u> words in each sentence to make the sentences true.

1 The correct casket is the one which is made of <u>gold</u>.
2 Portia gives Bassanio a valuable <u>jewel</u>.
3 Bassanio is very <u>worried</u> to see Lorenzo, Jessica, and Salarino in Belmont.
4 Portia says she can give Bassanio <u>advice</u> to solve Antonio's problem for him.
5 Antonio's letter explains that all his <u>friends</u> have been lost at sea.

Read Chapter 11. Are these sentences true or false?

1 Bassanio and Gratiano go to Venice by road.
2 Lorenzo is grateful to Portia for helping Antonio.
3 Portia tells Lorenzo her whole plan in detail.
4 Portia's cousin, Dr Bellario, lives in Rome.
5 Nerissa and Portia plan to be in disguise the next time they see their husbands.
6 Jessica and Lorenzo enjoy looking after Portia's house.

Read Chapter 12. Match the sentence halves.

1 The Duke begs Shylock …
2 Portia and Nerissa are so well disguised …
3 At first, Shylock is delighted …
4 Portia asks Shylock to accept three times the debt …
5 Shylock is ready to cut Antonio's flesh, …

a in return for tearing up the bond.
b to be merciful to Antonio.
c when Portia holds up a hand to stop him.
d that even their husbands don't recognize them.
e by the young lawyer's wise words.

Read Chapter 13. Put the events in order.

a Portia refuses any payment from Bassanio and Antonio.
b A court official prevents Shylock from leaving the room.
c Antonio suggests he should take care of half of Shylock's wealth for Lorenzo and Jessica.
d Bassanio is persuaded to give Portia his ring.
e Shylock is told that his life depends on the Duke's mercy.

Read Chapter 14. Answer the questions about people in the story.

1 Who swears he will never break a promise to his wife again?
2 Who makes a promise for his friend?
3 Who threatens to kill the lawyer's clerk?
4 Who has some good news about three of Antonio's ships?
5 Who has a copy of Shylock's will for Lorenzo?

ACTIVITIES

After Reading

Vocabulary

1 Match the verbs below to the definitions (a–f).

1	claim	a	to cry loudly
2	glitter	b	to want something very much
3	desire	c	to make a serious promise
4	swear	d	to ask for something because it's yours
5	sob	e	to send liquid or food out from your mouth
6	spit	f	to shine brightly with small flashes of light

2 Complete the sentences with the words below.

bond   honourable   interest   masks   scales   trusts   will

1 Antonio doesn't like the fact that Shylock charges ... on any money he lends.

2 Lorenzo's friends put on ... for Bassanio's party, so it is more difficult for them to recognize each other.

3 Everyone knows Antonio is an ... person – he always repays his debts if he can.

4 A ... is prepared by a lawyer and signed by both lender and borrower.

5 When Jessica agrees to run away with Lorenzo, she ... him to take care of her in future.

6 Portia's father stated certain conditions in his ... .

7 Shylock has his ... ready in the courtroom, so that he can weigh out a pound of Antonio's flesh.

Grammar

1 **Complete the statements by characters from the story. Use the words in brackets to make passive infinitives. Which person is most likely to say each sentence?**

'Nerissa, I don't want us (to / recognize) by our husbands.'
'Nerissa, I don't want us to be recognized by our husbands.'

1 'Gratiano, we can't allow Antonio (to / murder) by that evil Shylock!'
2 'My lord the Duke, my ducats ought (to / return) to me at once!'
3 'Nerissa, a lot of work has (to / do) before we arrive at court.'
4 'My lord Bassanio, I don't want (to / employ) by Shylock any more!'
5 'Dearest Lorenzo, I didn't expect (to / marry) to you so very soon!'

2 **Complete the statements using the past form of the modal verbs. Use the words in brackets.**

Shylock (should / accept) Bassanio's offer to pay three times the bond.
Shylock should have accepted Bassanio's offer to pay three times the bond.

1 Antonio's remarks (must / offend) Shylock in the past.
2 Bassanio (shouldn't / get) so badly into debt.
3 Gratiano (can't / realize) his wife was in the courtroom.
4 Antonio (should / never / sign) Shylock's bond.
5 Stephano (must / understand) his mistress's plan when she sent him to Padua.
6 Portia's father (can't / trust) her judgement in finding a good husband.

Reading

1 **Read the quotes from Shakespeare's *The Merchant of Venice*. Match them to their meanings (a–d). Who said this, to whom?**

1 My purse, my person, my extremest means,
Lie all unlocked to your occasions.

2 Whiles we shut the gate upon one wooer,
Another knocks at the door.

3 Farewell, and if my fortune be not crossed,
I have a father, you a daughter, lost.

4 Let me choose:
For as I am, I live upon the rack.

a As one suitor leaves, another arrives.

b I want to do the contest now – it's too painful to wait any longer!

c Everything I have is yours if you need it.

d With a bit of good luck, we'll never see each other again.

2 **Read the questions first, and then scan the text to find the answers.**

1 What does this document deal with?
a) marriage   b) money   c) family problems

2 Who is borrowing the money?
a) Ralph Talbot   b) Luke Lotti   c) Joe Evans

3 What will the borrower lose if he can't pay his debt?
a) his house   b) £1,000   c) his job

I, *Luke Lotti, merchant, agree to lend the sum of one thousand pounds to Joe Evans, clerk. I, Joe Evans, promise to pay the money back by 30 September 1562. If I fail to do this, I will give my house to Luke Lotti. We both sign this in the presence of Ralph Talbot, lawyer, today 30 June 1562.*

Writing

1 **Put the lines of the poem in the correct order, using the punctuation to help you. Which words have a similar sound or rhyme?**

    a How is it made, how is it fed?
    b With looks and stares, and Fancy dies
    c Be sure you note my message well.
    d Tell me, where is Fancy bred,
    e Where it was born, and there it lies.
    f In the heart, or in the head?
    g It is created in the eyes,
    h I am here these words to tell;

2 **Read part of another poem. What are the two missing words (rhyming with 'chest')?**

    Welcome to the silver chest!
    Lords have come from east and ...
    Their bravery and their skill to ...

3 **Write your own poem, using the bullet points to help you.**

    1 Write about:
        • someone or something you love
        • something that happened to you recently
        • a problem that anyone could have
        • an exciting adventure which ends sadly

    2 Try using some of these rhymes:
        *stood/wood/could   hour/power/flower   day/way/grey
        thought/taught/sort   sigh/high/cry   head/said/dead
        mine/sign/line   go/low/know   rolled/hold/cold*

Speaking

1 **Read the conversation. Do you agree or disagree with the speakers' points?**

A Don't you think Bassanio was wrong to borrow all that money from Antonio?

B Well, as far as I'm concerned, that's what friends are for.

A Really? I feel it's a bad idea to lend money to your friends, or borrow from them either.

B Anyway, he needed money to impress Portia, didn't he?

A Surely she isn't the right girl for him if she's only interested in his money! Don't you agree?

2 **Look at the conversation in exercise 1. Underline all the words and phrases used when giving and asking for opinions.**

3 **Money is important to everyone in this story, but how important is it to you? What would you do if you were in these situations? Discuss your answers with a partner, practising the words and phrases from exercises 1 and 2.**

1 You owe a lot of money to a close friend, but you have no savings, no cash, and no income.

2 You want to marry someone who is extremely wealthy, but you feel you have no chance because you are poor.

3 You would like to borrow from a money-lender, but his stated conditions could put a friend of yours in danger.

4 Your family is desperate for money, and if you worked in another country for ten years, you could help them.

5 There is plenty of cash at work; you wonder whether to 'borrow' some, and hope you can pay it back later before anyone notices.

THE OXFORD BOOKWORMS LIBRARY

THE OXFORD BOOKWORMS LIBRARY is a best-selling series of graded readers which provides authentic and enjoyable reading in English. It includes a wide range of original and adapted texts: classic and modern fiction, non-fiction, and plays. There are more than 250 Bookworms to choose from, in seven carefully graded language stages that go from beginner to advanced level.

Each Bookworm is illustrated, and offers extensive support, including:

▸ a glossary of above-level words
▸ activities to develop language and communication skills
▸ notes about the author and story
▸ online tests

Each Bookworm pack contains a reader and audio.

6	**STAGE 6**	▸ 2500 HEADWORDS	▸ CEFR B2–C1
5	**STAGE 5**	▸ 1800 HEADWORDS	▸ CEFR B2
4	**STAGE 4**	▸ 1400 HEADWORDS	▸ CEFR B1–B2
3	**STAGE 3**	▸ 1000 HEADWORDS	▸ CEFR B1
2	**STAGE 2**	▸ 700 HEADWORDS	▸ CEFR A2–B1
1	**STAGE 1**	▸ 400 HEADWORDS	▸ CEFR A1–A2
S	**STARTER**	▸ 250 HEADWORDS	▸ CEFR A1

Find a full list of *Bookworms* and resources at
www.oup.com/elt/gradedreaders

If you liked this Bookworm, why not try...

Little Dorrit
CHARLES DICKENS

Arthur Clennam's father's recent death has thrown up a mystery, and Arthur is determined to get to the bottom of it.